AN ILLUSTRATED GUIDE TO THE
MODERN
US ARMY

AN ILLUSTRATED GUIDE TO THE
MODERN
US ARMY

Edited by Richard O'Neill

PRENTICE HALL PRESS
New York   London   Toronto   Sydney   Tokyo

A Salamander Book

Prentice Hall Press
Gulf + Western Building
One Gulf + Western Plaza
New York, New York 10023

An Arco Military Book

Published in 1986 by the Prentice
Hall Trade Division

Originally published in the United
Kingdom by Salamander Books Ltd.

Previously published in the United
States by Arco Publishing, Inc.

PRENTICE HALL PRESS and
colophon are registered trademarks
of Simon & Schuster, Inc.

Library of Congress Catalog
Card Number 83-83418

ISBN 0-668-06066-2

10 9 8 7 6 5 4 3 2

Contents

Credits

Editor: Richard O'Neill
Designer: Philip Gorton

Filmset: Modern Text Typesetting Ltd.

Printed: in Belgium by
Henri Proost et Cie.

Publisher's note: Some material in
this book has previously appeared in
Salamander's *The US War Machine*, and
we are grateful for the contributions
of Christopher F. Foss and Bill Gunston.
We also wish to thank the US Army
and other Department of Defense official
archives who have supplied photographs
for this book.

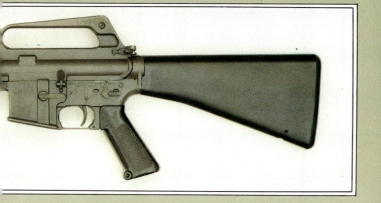

Introduction

The beginning of 1984 found the US Army with global commitments on an almost unprecedented scale. In Central America there are troops deployed in Panama (9,000) and Grenada (over 1,000), on exercise in Honduras (4,000), and advisers in El Salvador (56). In the Far East there are troops in Japan (2,400) and South Korea (27,397), while in the Middle East there are 1,220 in Egypt and 250 in Saudi Arabia. The major overseas concentration is in Western Europe (213,000), leaving some 525,000 troops in the USA itself. Of these last, 3⅓ divisions are "double-earmarked" to both the Rapid Deployment Force (RDF) and to NATO. As the world's troublespots seem to increase in number, the 783,000 men and women of the US Army seem to be spread ever more thinly, and General John A. Whickham, Army Chief of Staff, has recently warned that the "current US commitments probably exceed the force capabilities".

Geopolitical factors pose considerations which affect Army structure and doctrinal development, the most prominent being the problem of projecting military power abroad. Army planners need to be able to structure forces for possible deployment anywhere in the world, when the fundamental requirements of different areas, terrain, and types of warfare are quite dissimilar. Army assessments of possible military threats in the 1980s have led to two conclusions. One is that, given the technological and numerical realities, US forces cannot win by relying on attrition and a tactical doctrine based on defense. The second conclusion is that, while the Army must be organized and equipped to win on the conventional battlefield, it will also have to be prepared to respond to enemy-initiated use of chemical or nuclear weapons.

These conclusions prompted two new efforts which are having profound effects on the

AirLand Battle 2000

The US Army's most recent battle methodology is a totally new concept entitled AirLand Battle 2000. The central idea is a strategic defense of NATO's central region by aggressive tactics, which would include immediate, sustained and simultaneous attacks both in depth and on the line of contact.

Based on a 20-year Soviet threat projection, assessments conclude that the US Army, heavily outnumbered in both men and equipment, would be foolish to fight a war of attrition. Rather, the plan is for the Army to defend offensively, to strike quickly at Soviet assault echelons, while seeing subsequent echelons, in an attempt to finalize this stage of the battle before the enemy's follow-up armies join the fray. The intention is to attack the enemy throughout the depth of his formation with air, artillery and electronic means, and by use of high maneuverability. It is planned to confuse the enemy and cause him to fight in more than one direction, by deploying ground maneuver forces to the rear of his advance echelons. The Army will take advantage of the Soviet tactics which (as they exist today) mean there is an inevitable time-lag between follow-on echelons, such periods normally being lulls in the intense fighting. AirLand Battle tactics will upset the enemy's advance timetable, and force him to change his plans even to the

US Army. One is a tactical doctrine, the "AirLand Battle"; the other an organizational change to accommodate the new doctrine and weapons systems.
(continued on page 10)

▶

Above: The ideal military action has a clearly demonstrable aim and is quickly accomplished with minimal casualties. These US Army men in Grenada fulfilled all of these requirements in 1983.

extent of altering routes or splitting forces, so that hopefully subsequent defending forces will not have to face enemy forces too strong for them to defeat.

A scenario would have a US Army brigade attack the enemy's first echelon assault regiments while "seeing" the first echelon assault divisions. These are attacked by a US Army division, which at the same time "sees" the first echelon assault armies. These in turn are attacked by the US Army corps which must also disrupt the timetable of the second echelon divisions of the first echelon armies.

The depth attack, penetrating as much as 200 miles (321km), would be by fully integrated air forces (hence the air-land aspect), indirect fire systems, and by deep penetration ground units. The concept will entail small combat units which will operate relatively independently of each other. It also includes tactics for fighting in 360 degrees to meet the threat posed by the Warsaw Pact tactics; indeed, almost challenging them to attempt to surround the Army's agile combat forces. The concept will depend heavily on new technology, especially in communications, and in the rapid collection and assessment of intelligence data. Brigade commanders must know their superior commanders' intent, rather than have constant dialogue, thus combining the strategic and tactical levels.

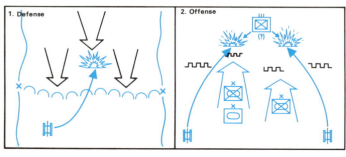

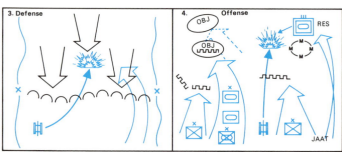

Basic Army Tactics

1—2: Delay of forces to prevent reinforcement

The first form of depth attack is used both when in defense (1) and in attack (2). The aim is to disrupt the enemy forces in depth, particularly the second echelon, to delay (or even prevent) their arrival in the battle area. This enables the enemy forces in contact to be isolated and then defeated in detail. Deception, offensive electronic warfare, artillery fire, counter-battery fire and air interdiction will all be used in this form of deep battle. The commander must decide when he needs particular enemy units isolated in this way.

3—4: Delay in enemy forces to allow maneuver completion

The second concept also involves attacking the enemy deep forces with fire. Its aim, however, is not so much to prevent the reinforcement of committed forces, as in (1) and (2) above, but rather to prevent them from interfering with own forces' attacks or counter attacks against the flanks or rear of enemy close-battle forces. Valuable targets in the deep battle may well prove to be different from those in the close-in battle; for example, bridges may be targets of higher value than tactical units when the aim is to prevent the arrival and deployment of the enemy's second echelon.

5—6: Decisive deep attack

The third form of tactical operation in this concept is both more complex and more difficult to achieve. It involves the engagement of the enemy follow-on echelon with both firepower and maneuver forces at the same time as the close-in battle continues. This is designed to stop the enemy from massing, to deprive him of momentum, and, most important of all, to destroy his force in its entirety. This will require the use of every combat and support element in close harmony. It will also require very close coordination between Army air and ground maneuver forces, artillery, electronic warfare, and Air Force battlefield interdiction.

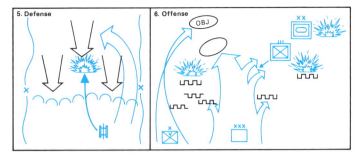

5. Defense

6. Offense

OBJ

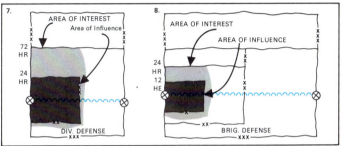

7. AREA OF INTEREST
Area of Influence

72 HR

24 HR

DIV. DEFENSE

8. AREA OF INTEREST

AREA OF INFLUENCE

24 HR
12 HE

BRIG. DEFENSE

7—8: Areas of influence and interest

The area of influence (7) is the operational area assigned to a commander within which he is capable of acquiring and fighting enemy units with assets organic to his command, plus any assigned to him in support of the particular operation. The size of the area will vary according to the prevailing conditions and the superior officer's plans. The latter also designates the front and flanking boundaries of the area. The area of interest (8) extends beyond the area of influence to include any enemy forces capable of affecting operations by the formation concerned.

9: Organization of the defense

The purpose of the defense is to provide an opportunity to gain the initiative, and commanders are expected to combine elements of static and dynamic tactical action. With this increased emphasis on offensive action and agility, reserve forces have become particularly important for counterattacks.

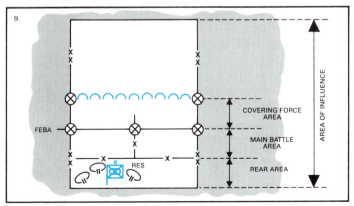

9.

COVERING FORCE AREA

MAIN BATTLE AREA

REAR AREA

AREA OF INFLUENCE

FEBA

RES

▶ US Army Tactical Doctrine

The principles of US Army tactical doctrine are influenced by economics, American attitudes, and the perceived threat. US and NATO strategists see the major threat as coming from the USSR and the Warsaw Pact and directed against Western Europe, and US land forces are structured to meet this. In an attack with little or no warning (the "cold-start" scenario) the Warsaw Pact has a numerical advantage in divisions, tanks, artillery, and aircraft. To counter this the US Army has developed qualitatively superior equipment and a tactical doctrine designed to defeat a numerically superior attacker. The new doctrine, promulgated in 1982, can be summarized as: to secure the initiative and exercise it aggressively to defeat the enemy. This inherently aggressive style is having far-reaching effects, and calls for greater use of maneuver and a greater recognition of human factors on the battlefield. There are four tenets derived from the operational concept: first, *Initiative,* ie, to cause the enemy to react to US forces rather than vice-versa; second, *Depth,* a three-dimensional combination of time, resources, and distance, which provides momentum in attack and elasticity in defense; third, *Agility,* which involves not only rapid mental and planning flexibility, but also acting faster than the enemy, described by one American general as "getting there firstest with the mostest"; fourth, *Synchronization,* a total unity of effort, with joint-Service and allied connotations. Implicit in this tenet is an awareness of higher commanders' intentions, so that all levels and activities are in pursuit of the same goals. ▶

Right: The essential raw material of any army is its soldiers. After Vietnam, there was some doubt about the quality and motivation of US soldiers, but their pride and self-confidence has been almost fully restored.

▶ Offensive Operations

Fundamental to the US Army's offensive operations are five principles—concentration, surprise, speed, flexibility, and audacity. *Concentration* to achieve local superiority followed by rapid dispersion to disrupt the enemy defensive efforts involves logistics as well as maneuver planning and execution. *Surprise* includes avoiding enemy strength and attacking his weaknesses. *Speed,* an element implicit in all of the concepts, is more than mere rapidity of movement, and includes any and all actions which promote the enemy's confusion as well as contributing to friendly maneuver. *Flexibility* in an environment where forces may cover 30 or more miles (50 or more km) a day, calls for the ability to exploit opportunities as they arise. *Audacity* recognizes risk but rejects tactical gamble.

Types of offensive operations describe the purpose rather than a method and have not changed from earlier listings: movement to contact—hasty attack—deliberate attack—exploitation —pursuit.

Movement to contact is intended to develop the situation while maintaining the commander's freedom of actions.

Hasty attacks are called for as a result of a meeting engagement or a successful defense.

Exploitation and *pursuit* follow successful attacks.

Right: US Army soldier (wearing the new helmet) aiming a Stinger missile. The gun versus missile argument has still not been settled in the air defense field.

Below: A Special Forces combat engineer about to blow a bridge. After a period of neglect, the Special Forces are now in great demand once again.

Defensive Operations

Changes in defense called for in the 1982 Operations Manual are more in spirit and operational style than mechanical or definitional. The defense is considered more a matter of purpose than form, with offensive combat characterizing operations. Commanders are expected to combine static and dynamic forms in light of their mission, terrain, relative strength, and mobility. In this context, "static" defense implies retention of particular terrain and tends to rely on fire power to destroy the enemy. "Dynamic" defense orients more on the enemy force than on retention of terrain objectives and tends to greater use of maneuver against attacking forces.

Heightened emphasis on rear area protection is a function of the increased demands on command and control systems as well as the high volume of fuel and ammunition consumption which the battlefield of the future will entail. Combat support and combat service support (logistics) units will be dispersed to avoid presenting lucrative targets but must be mutually supporting for possible rear area combat operations. Allocation of resources and placement takes into account the probabilities of enemy air mobile, nuclear, chemical and conventional air attack, along with such factors as sabotage and unconventional warfare.

The Corps

Organizational implications of the airland battle are extensive. All levels of operational forces must be modified to support the new doctrine and to accommodate the rapidly changing technology. The heavy corps design envisions operating with from $3\frac{2}{3}$ divisions to 5 divisions. A type corps will have a minimum strength of some 60,000 personnel and be capable of expansion as needed. Design considerations include provisions for coordination with allied forces and the increased operational participation with US Tactical Air Forces.

►

US Army Heavy Division

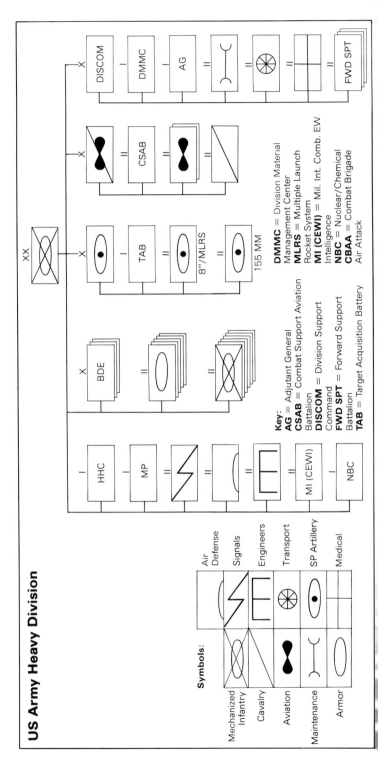

Key:
AG = Adjutant General
CSAB = Combat Support Aviation Battalion
DISCOM = Division Support Command
FWD SPT = Forward Support Battalion
TAB = Target Acquisition Battery

DMMC = Division Material Management Center
MLRS = Multiple Launch Rocket System
MI (CEWI) = Mil. Int. Comb. EW Intelligence
NBC = Nuclear/Chemical
CBAA = Combat Brigade Air Attack

Symbols:

Mechanized Infantry	Air Defense
Cavalry	Signals
Aviation	Engineers
Maintenance	Transport
Armor	SP Artillery
	Medical

▶ The Division

A total of 16 divisions make up the active army ground combat force. The division is the largest force that trains and fights as a combined arms team. It is a balanced, self-sustaining force that normally conducts operations as part of a larger force, but is capable of conducting independent operations, especially when supplemented by additional combat support and combat service support elements. Normally, the division fights as part of a corps, with three to five divisions making up the corps force. The division is designed to fight conventional operations, or a mixture of conventional and chemical-nuclear operations, in any part of the world.

While the division is the basic combined arms formation, the battalion is the basic maneuver unit, with normally three to five battalions comprising a brigade. Each division has three brigade headquarters to which battalions are assigned as the commander sees fit. The HQ of the Cavalry Brigade Air Attack also has the capability of controlling ground maneuver units which, in effect, gives the division an additional brigade level headquarters. Heavy maneuver battalions—armor and mechanized infantry—fight best in open country operations, in any part of the world, using terrain to maximum advantage. The light maneuver forces—rifle infantry, air assault infantry, airborne infantry, and ranger infantry—are ideally suited to more restricted terrain where close-in fighting becomes the norm.

The maneuver elements of the division are grouped together under brigade control in accordance with the terrain, the ▶

Current Division Forces

	Active Duty Div (Bdes)	Reserve Component Div (Bdes)
AR	4 (12)	2 (6)
Mech Infantry	6 (16) +2 Reserve	1 (3)
Infantry	4 (10) +2 Reserve	5 (15)
Air Assault	1 (3)	
Airborne	1 (3)	
Total Div (Bdes)	16 (44)	8 (24)
Separate Bde (Incl 4 RO)		
AR	1	4
Mech Infantry	1	7
Infantry	0	5
CBAC	1	0
Armored Cav Rgt	3	4
Theater Force Bdes	3	4
Total Separate Bdes	9	24

Below: American soldiers must be prepared to fight anywhere in the world, from Arctic to desert.

15

enemy they face, and the mission they must accomplish. Tank and mechanized infantry battalions rarely fight as pure organic units, but are cross-attached or task-organized by the brigade commanders to perform specific mission tasks to utilize more fully their capabilities and offset each other's vulnerabilities. The division commander allocates maneuver units to the brigade commanders, who in turn cross-attach these forces to optimize the weapon systems of each unit. The resultant battalion task forces are a combination of tank and mechanized infantry companies under the command of a battalion commander. A tank-heavy force would normally be structured to operate in open, rolling terrain, while the mechanized-infantry-heavy task force is better suited to operate in more restricted terrain and built-up areas. An even mix of tank and mechanized infantry results in a balanced task force that provides great flexibility to the commander. A balanced force would normally be structured when information about the enemy is vague or when the terrain is mixed and variable.

Because of global contingencies, US Army force structure provides for several types of divisions. In general terms, light divisions will have strengths of approximately 17,000. With transportability as a major factor, these divisions will rely on armor-defeating systems other than tanks, e.g. TOW missiles. Each division will have 9 or 10 infantry battalions and supporting units comparable to the heavy division but scaled to their lighter weaponry support requirements. Currently, it is anticipated that six divisions will be light (1 airborne, 1 air-mobile, 4 infantry), the remaining ten heavy.

Below: Post-storage proof firing of TOW missiles by soldiers of 1st Bn, 61st Infantry, at Fort Polk, La. TOW is one of the best anti-tank guided weapons (ATGWs) in the world.

Above: TOW missile is fired from the new M2 Bradley IFV; this is the vehicle upon which the US Army is pinning all its hopes.

Tank Battalion

The tank battalion has 565 officers and enlisted personnel organized into four tank companies and an HQ company. Each tank company has three platoons of four tanks each. Maintenance and support functions are consolidated in the battalion HQ company, as are a scout platoon and a six-tube mortar platoon. Current tank battalions have M60A3 or M1 Abrams tanks. The M60A3 has a 105mm gun which is highly effective at 2,190 yards (2,000m) and a cruising range of 310 miles (500km); the main gun is stabilized for firing on the move. The M1 Abrams tank is the newest system and will replace the M60 over the next few years. The new tank battalion is designed to employ 58 of the M1 tanks.

Tanks use their mobility and combat power to outflank the enemy or to penetrate the enemy defenses. Once armor has broken through to the enemy rear, it destroys or disrupts the enemy defenses in depth. Tanks are also well suited for rapid and dynamic exploitation and pursuit operations.

Mechanized Infantry Battalion

The mechanized infantry battalion has 880 officers and enlisted personnel organized into four mechanized rifle companies, an anti-armor company and an HQ company. The four-rifle-company configuration allows for cross-attachment with the similarly structured tank battalions. Each rifle company has three platoons of three squads each. Maintenance and support func- ▶

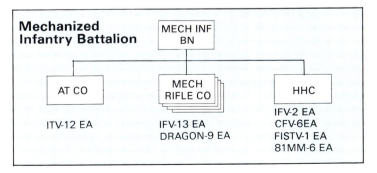

Mechanized Infantry Battalion

- MECH INF BN
  - AT CO — ITV-12 EA
  - MECH RIFLE CO — IFV-13 EA / DRAGON-9 EA
  - HHC — IFV-2 EA / CFV-6 EA / FISTV-1 EA / 81MM-6 EA

▶ tions are consolidated in the battalion HQ company, along with a scout platoon and a mortar platoon. The anti-armor company has three platoons of two sections each, and contains a total of 12 Improved TOW Vehicles. (The TOW has a 3,280 yards/3,000m range.) Each rifle company has 9 Dragon (1,093 yards/1,000m range) man-portable anti-armor guided missiles. The M2 Infantry Fighting Vehicle (IFV) is designed to provide infantry with cross-country mobility comparable to the Abrams tank.

The mechanized infantry usually operates as part of a combined arms force. The infantrymen remain mounted in their carriers until they are required to assault or forced to dismount by the enemy. The carriers displace to protected positions to provide supporting fire. The new IFVs will greatly enhance the infantryman's ability to fight while mounted and protected.

Cavalry Brigade Air Attack (CBAA)

This organization of approximately 1,700 officers and enlisted personnel is designed to consolidate the aviation assets of the division as well as to provide an additional control headquarters. In addition to its headquarters troop, the CBAA has two attack helicopter battalions, a combat support aviation battalion, and the division's cavalry squadron. Principal weapons of the attack helicopter

battalions are their 21 AAH and 13 OH-58C (observation) aircraft. The cavalry squadron has two air cavalry troops which also have AAH and OH-58C aircraft (4 AAH, 6 OH-58C each). The two ground cavalry troops each have 19 cavalry fighting vehicles. Aerial movement of personnel and equipment, maintenance of aircraft, and aerial observer support for the division artillery is provided by the combat support aviation battalion.

The AAH uses speed as well as natural and manmade cover and concealment (hills, trees, buildings, etc) to avoid enemy air defenses. Equipped with sights and night vision sensors, the two-man crew can navigate and attack in darkness or poor visibility. Upon sighting a target the AAH pops up from cover and fires one or more of its weapon systems. The weapons package for the AAH includes a 30mm chain gun, 2.75-inch rockets and the laser-homing Hellfire missile in various combinations.

The OH-58C, with its radar warning and heat suppression systems, provides a survivable observation capability which can operate at night.

Division Artillery

Some 3,000 strong, the division artillery organization follows traditional principles of direct support for the maneuver elements and a longer range capability to support the battle as a whole or general support. Each

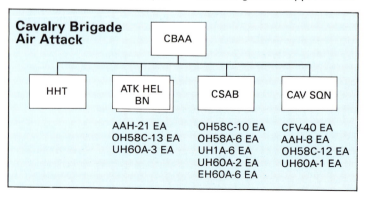

Cavalry Brigade Air Attack

CBAA

HHT	ATK HEL BN	CSAB	CAV SQN

ATK HEL BN:
AAH-21 EA
OH58C-13 EA
UH60A-3 EA

CSAB:
OH58C-10 EA
OH58A-6 EA
UH1A-6 EA
UH60A-2 EA
EH60A-6 EA

CAV SQN:
CFV-40 EA
AAH-8 EA
OH58C-12 EA
UH60A-1 EA

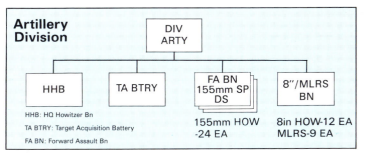

Artillery Division

```
                    ┌──────────┐
                    │   DIV    │
                    │   ARTY   │
                    └────┬─────┘
        ┌────────────┬───┴────────┬─────────────┐
   ┌────┴───┐  ┌─────┴────┐  ┌────┴─────┐  ┌─────┴────┐
   │        │  │          │  │ FA BN    │  │          │
   │  HHB   │  │ TA BTRY  │  │ 155mm SP │  │ 8"/MLRS  │
   │        │  │          │  │   DS     │  │   BN     │
   └────────┘  └──────────┘  └──────────┘  └──────────┘
```

HHB: HQ Howitzer Bn
TA BTRY: Target Acquisition Battery
FA BN: Forward Assault Bn

155mm HOW -24 EA

8in HOW-12 EA
MLRS-9 EA

155mm self-propelled howitzer battalion routinely supports one of the division's brigades. These battalions are fully mobile and can split their component batteries into two sections capable of independent operation. The general support battalion with its 8-inch howitzers and Multiple Launch Rocket Systems (MLRS) provides the division with an organic rocket capability as well as longer range weapons to fight the Deep Battle envisioned in the new tactical doctrine.

While the division 86 artillery has more guns than previous organizations, it is the improved responsiveness and flexibility which contributes most to its battlefield potency. Additional ammunition resupply capacity, additional fire direction capability, and the integration of automated systems to speed key functions, all increase artillery accuracy, lethality, and responsiveness. ▶

Below: The Multiple Launch Rocket System (MLRS) will become a virtual NATO standard weapons system. It fires 12 rockets with an 18-mile range.

▶ **Deployment Considerations**

Recent Soviet demonstrations of the capability and willingness to project military power have caused some re-evaluation of deployment considerations for US forces. Heavier tanks and infantry fighting vehicles and a host of mechanized supporting systems will significantly enhance the fire power and mobility of deployed forces in Europe, but will also significantly increase the strategic airlift and sealift required to move reinforcing units across the Atlantic.

In case of conflict between NATO and the Warsaw Pact, several factors combine to alleviate deployment problems. The existence of a forward base and depot structure in place in Europe, coupled with recent agreements between the United States and its European NATO allies, will reduce initial requirements to deploy logistical support forces. The commitment of European civilian ships and aircraft to the deployment effort will further ease the burden on US capabilities. Finally, the advantage enjoyed by NATO forces in terms of familiarity with the terrain, established command and control systems, and exercise experience, combine to offer a high degree of assurance that timely reinforcement of Europe is feasible.

Similar circumstances, combined with reduced requirements for armor and mechanized forces, apply to Korea, although the distances involved are far greater.

No such advantages are currently found, however, when possible contingency requirements for other potential areas of conflict are considered. The wide range of contingencies is reflected in the combat forces identified for employment with the Rapid Deployment Force (RDF), which include the 24th Mechanized Division, the 82nd Airborne Division, the 101st Air Assault Division, the 6th Cavalry Brigade (Air Combat), plus Ranger, Special Forces, and support forces. This does not mean that all of these units would be committed to all RDF contingencies, merely that a wide mix of heavy and light forces is available for tailoring packages of Army, Air Force, Navy, and Marine elements to meet specific circumstances, as happened, for example, in the Grenada operation.

The Army National Guard and the Army Reserve

There are two elements of the Total Army which must not be overlooked: the Army National Guard (ARNG) and the Army Reserve. The ARNG reached a paid strength of 417,019, which represents some 46 per cent of the Total Army, at the end of FY 1983. In unit terms, the ARNG provides 33 per cent of the combat divisions, almost 50 per cent of infantry, armor, and artillery battalions, and nearly 30 per cent of the combat support units. Although some ARNG equipment is old and difficult to maintain, recent changes in priority mean that the National Guard will shortly receive such modern equipment as the UH-60 and

US Ground Launched Tactical Nuclear Weapons Deployed in Europe

Name	No. of Launchers	Range miles (km)	Yield of Warhead	Year first deployed
Pershing[1]	108	280 (450)	60-400 Kt	1962
Lance	36	43-68 (70-110)	1-100 Kt	1972
8in howitzer M110A2	56	19 (20)	sub-to-low Kt	1962
155mm howitzer M109A2	252	15 (24)	sub-to-low Kt	1964

Source: *The Military Balance 1982-83* (IISS).
1. Pershing II deployed 1983 has a 1,120-mile (1,800km) range.

AH-1S helicopters, M1 and M60A3 MBTs, and the squad automatic weapon (SAW).

The Army Reserve was 269,000 strong at the end of FY 1983. Its units are mainly in the combat support, combat service support, and general support roles, while there are also many officers and soldiers in the Individual Ready Reserve. Some 12,000 troops of the Army Reserve are an integral part of the RDF, providing transport, fuel, and civil affairs support. If mobilization was to be ordered, some 20 per cent of the Army Reserve would be committed within 30 days, a total of 57 per cent within 30 to 60 days, and virtually 100 per cent within 90 days.

Conclusion

The US Army is a large and complex military organization with extensive responsibilities. It bore the brunt of the Vietnam experience, but the recovery is now virtually complete. Like other Western military forces, the US Army has assumed that a quantitative disadvantage

Above: These men of the US Army Reserve are an integral part of mobilization plans.

against the Warsaw Pact could be offset by Western technological superiority. There is, however, a growing realization that this can no longer be relied upon. Indeed, the US Army has suffered some major technical setbacks and difficulties. It has, for example, taken almost two decades to find successors to the M60 MBT and M113 APC, with many failures and much loss of time and waste of resources along the way. Some programs, such as the M60A2, M551 Sheridan, and Copperhead, have simply failed to fulfill the spectacular promises held out.

Despite all this, the US Army has some fine equipment and this book shows some of it. Inevitably, not all can be shown, and the selections have in some cases had to be a little arbitrary. Nevertheless, it is hoped that this book gives an overall picture of the equipment of a mighty fighting force.

Main Battle Tanks

The Main Battle Tank (MBT) is the linchpin of the US Army's plans for the land battle, although it could, of course, only be deployed as part of a combined arms force. It must certainly be at the core of the new and more aggressive tactics now promulgated in the AirLand Battle concept.

M1 Abrams

Type: Main battle tank.
Crew: 4.
Armament: One 105mm M68 gun; one 7·62mm machine gun co-axial with main armament; one 0·5in machine gun on commander's cupola; one M240 7·62mm machine gun on loader's hatch (see text).
Armor: Classified.
Dimensions: Length (gun forward) 32ft 0½in (9·766m); length (hull) 25ft 11¾in (7·918m); width 11ft 11¾in (3·655m); height 7ft 9½in (2·375m).
Weight: 120,000lb (54,432kg).
Engine: Avco Lycoming AGT-T 1500 HP-C turbine developing 1,500hp.
Performance: Road speed 45mph (72·4km/h); range 275 miles (443km); vertical obstacle 4ft 1in (1·244m); trench 9ft (2·743m); gradient 60 per cent.
History: First production vehicle completed in 1980.

In June 1973 contracts were awarded to both the Chrysler Corporation (which builds the M60 series) and the Detroit Diesel Allison Division of the General Motors Corporation (which built the MBT-70) to build prototypes of a new tank designated M1, and later named the Abrams tank. These tanks were handed over to the US Army for trials in February 1976. In November 1976 it was announced after a four-month delay that the Chrysler tanks would be placed in production. Production, which commenced at the Lima Army Tank Plant in Lima, Ohio, in 1979, with the first vehicles being completed the following year, is now also under way at the Detroit Arsenal Tank plant, which, like Lima, is now operated by the Land Systems Division ▶

Development of the US MBT has proved time-consuming and costly, and the M1 is only just starting to enter service. With this tank the US Army has overtaken Soviet tank technology after at least a decade in which it has lagged sadly behind. Despite the advent of the long-awaited M1, the M60 and M48 will remain in service in their improved versions for many years to come; indeed, production of the M60A3 has not yet ended. All US Army MBTs currently are armed with a 105mm gun, although the British and West Germans use 120mm and the USSR 125mm. The US will not be equipped with 120mm guns until the M1E1, with a West German gun, comes into service.

Above: The M1 Abrams main battle tank has taken many years to reach combat units but is now in service in very considerable numbers.

Far left: A prototype M1 fires its British-designed 105mm rifled main armament. From 1985 the M1E1 will be fitted with a German 120mm.

Left: An M1 lands after leaping an obstacle. The US Army intends that this MBT will set new standards in agility on the battlefield.

Above: The M1 has a 27 per cent lower silhouette than the M60A1 but with the same ground clearance of about 19 inches (48cm).

▶ of General Dynamics who took over Chrysler Defense Incorporated in 1982. By late 1982 over 600 M1s had been built and the tank is now entering service at an increasingly rapid rate. The first units to field the M1 were the three armored battalions of 3rd Infantry Division (Mechanized) who proudly gave the tank its European debut in 'Exercise Reforger' in August 1982. The US Army has a requirement for some 7,058 M1s by the end of Fiscal Year 1989. From 1985 it is expected that the 105mm M68 rifled tank gun will be replaced by the 120mm Rheinmetall smooth bore gun which is being produced under the designation XM256; this will fire both West German and American ammunition, although there have been more problems in adapting the turret to take the West German gun than had been anticipated.

The M1 has a hull and turret of the new British Chobham armor, which is claimed to make the tank immune to attack from all shaped-charge warheads and to give dramatically increased protection against other anti-tank rounds, including kinetic energy (i.e., APDS and APFSDS). It has a crew of four; the driver at the front, the commander and gunner on the right of the turret, and the loader on the left. The main armament consists of a standard 105mm gun developed in Britain and produced under license in the United States and a 7·62mm machine-gun is mounted co-axially with the main armament. A 0·5in machine-gun is mounted at the commander's station and a 7·62mm machine-gun at the loader's station. Ammunition supply consists of 55 rounds of 105mm, 1,000 rounds of 12·7mm and 11,400 rounds of 7·62mm. Mounted each side of the turret is a bank of six ▶

Above: The gunner's position inside the turret of the M1. The ever increasing sophistication of MBTs is leading to spiralling costs.

Below: An early-issue M1 Abrams moves through a village in West Germany. Current production is running at some 60 tanks per month.

▶ British-designed smoke dischargers. The main armament can be aimed and fired on the move. The gunner first selects the target, and then uses the laser rangefinder to get its range and then depresses the firing switch. The computer makes the calculations and adjustments required to ensure a hit.

The fuel tanks are separated from the crew compartment by armored bulkheads and sliding doors are provided for the ammunition stowage areas. Blow-out panels in both ensure that an explosion is channeled outward. The suspension is of torsion-bar type with rotary shock absorbers. The tank can travel across country at a speed of 30mph (48km/h) and accelerate from 0 to 20mph (0 to 32km/h) in seven seconds, and this will make the M1 a difficult tank to engage on the battlefield. The M1 is powered by a turbine developed by Avco Lycoming, running on a variety of fuels including petrol, diesel and jet fuel. All the driver has to do is adjust a dial in his compartment. According to the manufacturers, the engine will not require an overhaul until the tank has traveled between 12,000 to 18,000 miles (19,312 to 28,968km), a great advance over existing tank engines. This engine is coupled to an Allison X-1100 transmission with four forward and two reverse gears. Great emphasis has been placed on reliability and maintenance, and it is claimed that the complete engine can be removed for replacement in under 30 minutes. ▶

Right: Half the M1 production run will have the M68 105mm main gun seen here; the remainder will have a West German 120mm smoothbore.

Below: The M1 represents a major addition to the US Army's combat strength; 7,058 are on order at a current cost of $1·84 million each.

▶ The M1 is provided with an NBC system and a full range of night-vision equipment for the commander, gunner and driver.

It is not often realized that there are hundreds of sub contractors to a major program such as a tank. On the Chrysler M1 there are eight major subcontractors: the government for the armament, Avco Lycoming for the

Below: The M1 is powered by an Avco-Lycoming gas-turbine engine which develops 1,500hp. Fuel consumption has been criticized by some, but the tank has a range of 275 miles (443km) at a speed of 30mph (48km/h) on secondary roads, and can operate for a 24-hour combat day without needing to refuel.

engine, Cadillac Gage for the turret drive and the stabilization system, the Control Data Corporation for the ballistic computer, the Detroit Diesel Allison Division of General Motors for the transmission and the final drive, the Hughes Aircraft Company for the laser rangefinder, the Kollmorgen Corporation for the gunner's auxiliary sight and the Singer Kearfott Division for the line-of-sight data link.

Those Europeans who criticize the Americans for failing to make the "two-way street" a reality need look no farther than the M1. This epitome of the US Army's might has British armor, main gun, and smoke dischargers, and a Belgian 7·62mm machine gun, while later versions will convert to a West German main gun.

M48

M48A5, M67, M67A1, M67A2, M48 AVLB

Type: Medium tank.

Crew: 4.

Armament: One 105mm M68; one 0·3in M1919A4E1 machine gun co-axial with the main armament (some have a 7·62mm M73 MG); one 0·5in machine gun in commander's cupola.

Armor: 12·7mm-120mm (0·50-4·8in).

Dimensions: Length (including main armament) 28·3ft (8·686m); length (hull) 22ft 7in (6·882m); width 11ft 11in (3·631m); height (including cupola) 10ft 3in (3·124m).

Weight: Combat 108,000lb (48,989kg).

Ground pressure: 11·80lb/in^2 (0·83kg/cm^2).

Engine: Continental AVDS-1790-2A 12-cylinder air-cooled diesel developing 750hp at 2,400rpm.

Performance: Road speed 30mph (48km/h); range 288 miles (463km); vertical obstacle 3ft (0·915m); trench 8ft 6in (2·59m); gradient 60 per cent.

History: Entered service with the US Army in 1953. Used by Germany, Greece, Iran, Israel, Jordan, Lebanon, Morocco, Norway, Pakistan, Somalia, South Korea, Spain, Taiwan, Thailand, Tunisia, Turkey, United States and Vietnam. (*Specifications relate to M48A5 in US service.*)

Once the M47 was authorized for production, development started on a new medium tank, as the M47 was only a stop-gap measure. So in October 1950 Detroit Arsenal started design work on a new medium tank armed with a 90mm gun. This design study was completed two months later and in December 1950 Chrysler was given a contract to complete the design work and build six prototypes under the designation T48. The first of these prototypes had to be completed by December 1951. Production started in 1952 and first deliveries were made to the US Army the following year. The M48, as it was now called, was followed in production by the M60, essentially an M48A3 with a 105mm gun and other detailed changes, production of this model being undertaken at the Detroit Tank Plant.

　The hull of the M48 is of cast armor construction, as is the turret. The driver is seated at the front of the hull with the other three crew members located in the turret, with the commander and gunner on the right and the loader on the left. The engine and transmission are at the rear of the hull, and are separated from the fighting compartment by a fireproof bulkhead.

Below: Armored Vehicle Launched Bridge (AVLB) based on the M48 chassis. The bridge is 63ft (19·2m) long and weighs some 32,000lb.

Above: M48 with an M68 105mm gun undergoing tests (but not flamethrowing). The basic design is well over 30 years old.

The suspension is of the torsion-bar type and consists of six road wheels, with the drive sprocket at the rear and the idler at the front. Depending on the model there are between three and five track-return rollers, and some models have a small track tensioning wheel between the sixth road wheel and the drive sprocket. The main armament consists of a 105mm gun with an elevation of $+19°$ and a depression of $-9°$, traverse being $360°$. A 0·3in M1919A4E1 machine-gun is mounted co-axially with the main armament. The cupola can be traversed through $360°$, and the machine-gun can be elevated from $-10°$ to $+60°$.

The M48 can be fitted with a dozer blade, if required, at the front of the hull. All M48s have infra-red driving lights and some an infra-red/white searchlight mounted over the main armament. The type can ford to a depth of 4ft (1·219m) without preparation or 8ft (2·438m) with the aid of a kit.

The first model to enter service was the M48, and this had a simple cupola for the commander, with the machine-gun mounted externally. The second model was the M48C, which was for training use only as it had a mild steel hull. The M48A1 was followed by the M48A2, which had many improvements including a fuel-injection system for the engine and larger capacity fuel tanks. The M48A2C was a slightly modified M48A2. The M48A3 was a significant improvement as this had a diesel engine, which increased the vehicle's operational range considerably, and a number of other modifications including a different fire-control system. Latest model is the M48A5, essentially an M48A1 or M48A2 with modifications including an M68 main 105mm gun, new tracks, a 7·62mm M60D co-axial machine-gun and a similar weapon on the loader's hatch, plus many other detail modifications. One interesting modification is the fitting of an Israeli-developed low-profile cupola.

Earlier M48A1, M48A2C and M48A3 in the US inventory (some 1,809 tanks) have been updated to M48A5 standard and serve with Army National Guard and Reserve units. Some M48A1 and M48A2 chassis are being used for the Sergeant York (*qv*), pending availability of M48A5s.

Three flamethrower tanks were developed: the M67 (using the M48A1 chassis), the M67A1 (using the M48A2 chassis) and the M67A2 (using the M48A3 chassis). Also in service is an M48 Armored Vehicle-Launched Bridge. This has a scissors bridge which can be laid over gaps up to 60ft (18·288m) in width.

M60

M60, M60A1, M60A3, M60 AVLB, M728 CEV

Type: Main battle tank.
Crew: 4.
Armament: One 105mm gun; one 7·62mm machine gun co-axial with main armament; one 0·5in anti-aircraft machine gun in commander's cupola.
Armor: 12·7mm-120mm (0·5-4·80in).
Dimensions: Length (gun forward) 30ft 11in (9·436m); length (hull) 22ft 9½in (6·946m); width 11ft 11in (3·631m); height 10ft 8in (3·257m).
Weight: Combat 114,600lb (51,982kg).
Ground pressure: 11·24lb/in² (0·79kg/cm²).
Engine: Continental AVDS-1790-2A 12-cylinder diesel developing 750bhp at 2,400rpm.
Performance: Road speed 30mph (48km/h); range 280 miles (450km); vertical obstacle 3ft (0·914m); trench 8ft 6in (2·59m); gradient 60 per cent.
History: The M60 entered service with the US Army in 1960 and is also used by Austria, Egypt, Ethiopia, Iran, Israel, Italy, Jordan, Morocco, Saudi Arabia, Somalia, South Korea, Tunisia, Turkey, US Marine Corps, Yemen Arab Republic (North). (*Specifications relate to M60A3 model.*)

In the 1950s the standard tank of the United States Army was the M48. In 1957 an M48 series tank was fitted with a new engine for trials purposes and this was followed by another three prototypes in 1958. Late in 1958 it was decided to arm the new tank with the British 105mm L7 series gun, to be built in the United States under the designation M68. In 1959 the first production order for the new tank, now called the M60, was placed with Chrysler, and the type entered production at Detroit Tank Arsenal in late 1959, with the first production tanks being completed the following year.

From late in 1962, the M60 was replaced in production by the M60A1, which had a number of improvements, the most important being the redesigned turret. The M60A1 had a turret and hull of all-cast construction. The driver is seated at the front of the hull with the other three crew members in the turret, commander and gunner on the right and the loader on the left. The engine and transmission are at the rear, the latter having one reverse and two forward ranges. The M60 has torsion-bar suspension and six road wheels, with the idler at the front and the drive sprocket at the rear; there are four track-return rollers. The 105mm gun has an elevation of ▶

Below: A row of M60A3 MBTs with their turrets reversed. The gun is the M68 105mm. When production finishes in 1984/85 some 10,600 M60s will have been built, of which the US Army has 7,347.

Above: An M60 on exercise. The device on the barrel is a simulator which emits smoke when activated by an "enemy" tank with a laser.

Right: This shot of an M60A3 clearly shows the considerable height of the tank—10ft 8in (3·257m)—which is one of its main drawbacks. The good ballistic shaping of the turret is also clearly shown.

▶ +20° and a depression of –10°, and traverse is 360°. Both elevation and traverse are powered. A 7·62mm M73 machine-gun is mounted co-axially with the main armament and there is a 0·5in M85 machine-gun in the commander's cupola. The latter can be aimed and fired from within the turret, and has an elevation of +60° and a depression of –15°. Some 60 rounds of 105mm, 900 rounds of 0·5in and 5,950 rounds of 7·62mm ammunition are carried. Infra-red driving lights are fitted as standard and an infra-red/white light is mounted over the main armament. All M60s have an NBC system. The tank can also be fitted with a dozer blade on the front of the hull. The M60 can ford to a depth of 4ft (1·219m) without preparation or 8ft (2·438m) with the aid of a kit. For deep fording operations a schnorkel can be fitted, allowing the M60 to ford to a depth of 13ft 6in (4·14m). ▶

Above: An M60 of the US Army in West Germany. "On-the-spot" training ensures maximum combat readiness.

▶   The M60A2 was a special model armed with a 152mm gun/launcher but has now been phased out of service. Current production model is the M60A3 with numerous improvements including stabilization of main armament, top loading air cleaner fitted, passive searchlight over main armament, new tracks with removable pads, tube over bar suspension, RISE engine, thermal sleeve for main armament, laser rangefinder, passive night vision devices, new MAG 7·62mm MG, smoke dischargers each side of turret, muzzle reference system, engine smoke dischargers and improved personnel heater. Most M60A1s of the US Army are now being brought up to this new standard, with the aim of an M60A3 fleet totalling 7,347

Below: A total of 526 M60A2s was built at Detroit in the 1960s, but due to many problems the tank did not enter service until 1975.

Above: M60 MBTs cross a floating bridge on exercise. Such sights will become rarer as M60 is replaced by M1.

(1,686 from new production and 5,661 from conversion of M60A1s in Army depots). Of these, 3,786 will be the M60A3 TTS version, which has all the improvements listed above, plus a tank thermal sight. By 1981 total production of the M60 series of MBTs had amounted to over 10,600 vehicles with final vehicles scheduled to be completed in 1983. Specialized versions of the M60 series include the M60 armored vehicle launched bridge and the M728 Combat Engineer Vehicle which is fitted with a bulldozer blade, 152mm demolition gun and an A-frame for lifting obstacles which is pivoted at the front of the hull. The basic vehicle can also be fitted with roller type mineclearing equipment or a dozer blade.

Below: One of the many specialized versions of the M60 is the M728 Combat Engineer Vehicle, with bulldozer blade and 6in (152mm) gun.

Armored Personne Carriers

With the M113 the US Army set the pattern for a simple, tracked, armored box (a "battle taxi") which has been followed by most Free World armies for two decades. After many years of indecision and confusion—and some costly

M2/M3

Type: (M2) Infantry fighting vehicle; (M3) Cavalry fighting vehicle.
Crew: 3 plus 6.
Armament: One 25mm Hughes "chain-gun"; one 7·62mm machine-gun co-axial with main armament; twin launcher for Hughes TOW ATGW.
Armor: Classified.
Dimensions: Length 21ft 2in (6·45m); width 10ft 6in (3·20m); height 9ft 9in (2·97m).
Weight: 50,000lb (22,680kg).
Ground pressure: 7·7lb/in² (0·54kg/cm²).
Engine: Cummins (VTA-903T water-cooled 4-cycle diesel developing 506bhp.
Performance: Road speed 41mph (66km/h); water speed 4·5mph; range 300 miles (384km); vertical obstacle 3ft (0·91m); trench 8ft 4in (2·54m); gradient 60 per cent.
History: Entered US Army service in 1983.

Below: An M2 Bradley Infantry Fighting Vehicle (IFV) at speed, showing its excellent agility, which equates with that of the M1 MBT.

mistakes—the M2 Infantry Combat Vehicle is at last entering service. It is fast, well protected, heavily armed, and enables the mounted infantry to fire weapons (albeit over a limited arc) from inside the vehicle. It is also heavy (over 22 tons), very expensive, and has reduced the effective size of the infantry squad to six men. Indeed, the tactical use of the M2 and of its dismounted squad do not seem to have been fully defined as yet, some crucial decisions having been left until the new vehicle is actually in service. Even when the M2 is in full service many thousands of M113s will remain in front-line units as weapons carriers and as communications and headquarters vehicles.

The United States Army has had a requirement for an MICV for well over 15 years. The first American MICV was the XM701, developed in the early 1960s on the M107/M110 self-propelled gun chassis. This proved unsatisfactory during trials. The Americans then tried to modify the current M113 to meet the MICV role: a variety of different models was built and tested, but again these vehicles failed to meet the army requirement. As a result of a competition held in 1972, the FMC Corporation, which still builds the M113A2, was awarded a contract to design an MICV designated the XM723. The XM723 did not meet the requirements of the US Army and further development, based on the same chassis, resulted in the Fighting Vehicle System (FVS) which comprised two vehicles, the XM2 Infantry Fighting Vehicle and the XM3 Cavalry Fighting Vehicle. These were eventually accepted for service as the M2 and M3 Bradley Fighting Vehicles. The US Army has a requirement for some 6,882 M2/M3 vehicles, and three battalions of M2s were formed in 1983, the first at Ford Hood, Texas.

The primary task of the M2 in the eyes of the US Army is to enable infantry to fight from under armor whenever practicable, and to be able both to observe and to use their weapons from inside the vehicle. The M2 ▶

Below: An infantry squad "debussing" from its M2. The small size of the crew compartment has reduced the dismounting squad to six.

Above: M2 IFV with twin launcher for TOW ATGWs in the traveling position alongside the two-man turret. M231 rifles are not fitted.

Left: M2 on a road-test. Note the splash-board resting on the glacis plate and the steel armor on the vehicle side for added protection.

▶ will replace some, but not all, of the current M113 APCs, as the latter are more than adequate for many roles on the battlefield. The M2 has three major advances over the existing M113 APC. First, the IFV has greater mobility and better cross-country speed, enabling it to keep up with the M1 MBT when acting as part of the tank/infantry team. Second, it has much greater firepower. Third, it has superior armor protection. The tank provides long-range firepower whilst the IFV provides firepower against softer, close-in targets. The M2's infantry also assist tanks by locating and destroying enemy anti-tank weapons.

The hull of the M2 is of all-welded aluminum construction with an applique layer of steel armor welded to the hull front, upper sides and rear for added protection. The hull sides also have a thin layer of steel armor, the ▶

41

Above: M2 Bradley IFV on the firing range. Note the box on the near-side of the turret which is a twin TOW anti-tank missile launcher.

Above: An M2 on a cross-country driving course. Main gun is a Hughes 25mm "Chain-Gun"; to its right is 7·62mm coaxial MG.

Left: An M2 launches a TOW missile. The armament on the M2 IFV will add substantially to the firepower available to infantry battalions.

▶ space between the aluminum and steel being filled with foam to increase the buoyancy of the vehicle. The armored protection of the IFV is claimed to be effective against Soviet 14·5mm armor-piercing rounds and 155mm air-burst shell splinters.

The driver is seated at the front of the vehicle on the left, with the engine to his right. The two-man turret is in the center of the hull and the personnel compartment is at the rear. Personnel entry is effected through a large power-operated ramp in the hull rear. The two-man power operated turret is fully stabilized and is armed with a 25mm Hughes Chain Gun and a co-axial 7·62mm machine gun. The weapons can be elevated to +60° and depressed to −10°, turret traverse being 360°. Mounted on the left side of the turret is a twin launcher for the Hughes TOW ATGW. A total of 900 rounds of 25mm, 2,340 rounds of 7·62mm and seven TOW missiles are carried. The troop compartment is provided with six firing ports (two in each side and two at the rear) for the 5·56mm M231 weapon. The M231 is a specially developed version of the M16, cut-down and sealed in a ball mount. It is somewhat ironic that the outcome of a requirement for the infantry to be able to use their weapons from inside the vehicle should be an additional and specialized rifle. Three M72A2 light anti-tank weapons are also carried. The M2 is fully amphibious, although a flotation screen is required, and is propelled in the water by its tracks. An NBC system is fitted, as is a full range of night vision equipment.

Some 3,300 M3 Cavalry Fighting Vehicles are to be purchased to replace M60s and M113s in armored cavalry units and in the scout platoons of mechanized infantry and tank battalions. The M3 is outwardly identical with the M2: the major differences lie in the internal stowage and the layout of the crew compartment. The M3 carries twice the number of stowed 25mm rounds and ten stored TOW missiles. Only two cavalrymen are housed in the rear compartment and the firing ports are not used.

The chassis of the M2/M3 is also used as the basis for the Vought Multiple Launch Rocket System and the Armored, Forward-Area, Rearm Vehicle (AFARV) which has been designed to supply MBTs with ammunition when they are in the battlefield area.

M113A2

M113, M113A1, M113A2, M106, M132, M163 and variants.

Type: Armored personnel carrier.
Crew: 2 plus 11.
Armament: One Browning 0·5in (12·7mm) machine-gun.
Armor: 12mm-38mm (0·47-1·58in).
Dimensions: Length 15ft 11in (4·863m); width 8ft 10in (2·686m); height 8ft 2in (2·5m).
Weight: Combat 24,600lbs (11,156kg).
Ground Pressure: 7·82lb/in² (0·55kg/cm²).
Engine: General Motors Model 6V53 six-cylinder water-cooled diesel developing 215bhp at 2,800rpm.
Performance: Road speed 42mph (67·6km/h); water speed 3·6mph (5·8km/h); range 300 miles (483km); vertical obstacle 2ft (0·61m); trench 5ft 6in (1·68m); gradient 60 per cent.
History: Entered service with the United States Army in 1960. Also used by 50 other countries.

In the early 1950s the standard United States Army APC was the M75, followed in 1954 by the M59. Neither of these was satisfactory and in 1954 foundations were laid for a new series of vehicles. In 1958 prototypes of the T113 (aluminum hull) and T117 (steel hull) armored personnel carriers were built. A modified version of the T113, the T113E1, was cleared for production in mid-1959 and production commenced at the FMC plant at San Jose, California, in 1960. The vehicle is still in production today and some 70,000 have been built in the USA. It is also built in Italy by Oto Melara, which has produced a further 4,000 for the Italian Army and for export. In 1964 the M113 was replaced in production by the M113A1, identical with the earlier model but for a diesel rather than a petrol engine.

The M113A1 had a larger radius of action than the earlier vehicle. The M113 had the distinction of being the first armored fighting vehicle of ▶

Below: The squat shape of the M113 is distinctive even amidst the snows of Alaska, as a squad from Company A, 1st BG, 23rd Infantry, goes through a tactical demonstration at the Fort Richardson training aids area.

Above: More M113 chassis have been built than any other since 1945. This is the M557 unarmed command post version.

Below: M113s in convoy through a German town during "Autumn Reforger" NATO exercises in 1982. It is the standard personnel carrier in mechanized infantry units but, unable to keep pace with the M1 tank, will be replaced by the M2 IFV.

aluminum construction to enter production. The driver is seated at the front of the hull on the left, with the engine to his right. The commander's hatch is in the center of the roof and the personnel compartment is at the rear of the hull. The infantry enter and leave via a large ramp in the hull rear, although there is also a roof hatch over the troop compartment. The basic vehicle is normally armed with a pintle-mounted Browning 0·5in machine-gun, which has 2,000 rounds of ammunition. The M113 is fully amphibious and is propelled in the water by its tracks. Infra-red driving lights are fitted as standard. FMC has developed a wide variety of kits for the basic vehicle including an ambulance kit, NBC kit, heater kit, dozer-blade kit, various shields for machine-guns and so on.

The current production model is the M113A2 which is essentially an M113A1 with improved engine cooling and improved suspension. Most US Army M113 and M113A1 vehicles are now being brought up to M113A2 standard.

There are more variants of the M113 family than any other fighting vehicle in service today, and there is room here to mention only some of the ▶

Left: The M901 Improved TOW Vehicle (ITV), whose missile components can be removed for ground-launching if tactically necessary.

Below: The M730 Chaparral launcher is a variant of the M548, based on the M113 chassis.

Above: One of the many derivatives of the basic M113 is this XM981 Fire-Support Team Vehicle (FIST-V) for artillery forward observers.

Right: M548A1 cargo carrier is based on the M113 and is widely used in the US Army for a variety of load-carrying tasks.

▶ more important models. The M577 is the command model, with a much higher roof and no armament. There are two mortar carriers: the M125 with an 81mm mortar, and the M106 with a 107mm mortar. The flame-thrower model is known as the M132A1, and is not used outside the United States Army. The M806 is the recovery model, and this is provided with a winch in the rear of the vehicle and spades at the rear. The anti-aircraft model is known as the Vulcan Air Defense System or M163; this is armed with a six-barrelled 20mm General Electric cannon. The M548 tracked cargo carrier is based on an M113 chassis, can carry 5 tons (5,080kg) of cargo and is fully amphibious. There are many models of the M548, including the M727, which carries three HAWK surface-to-air missiles, and the M730, which carries four Chaparral short-range surface-to-air missiles. Yet another version, the M752, carries the Lance tactical missile system, whilst the M688 carries two spare missiles.

One recent model is the M901 Improved TOW Vehicle (ITV), with a retractable launcher that carries two Hughes TOW ATGWs in the ready-to-launch position. Almost 2,000 of these vehicles have been ordered by the US Army. The latest model to be ordered is the Surface-Launched Unit Fuel-Air Explosive (SLUFAE) launcher, which is an unguided rocket system based on the M548 chassis.

The M113 series and its derivatives will remain in service with the US and foreign armies for many years to come. Like the "Jeep" of World War II, it is cheap, simple to manufacture, easy to maintain, and effective in use. The US Army may well one day wish that the same applied to the M2/M3 series.

Above: An infantry squad debussing from an M113, virtually the standard APC in Western-oriented armies since the 1960s.

Reconnaissance Vehicles

The US Army has put more emphasis than most other armies on the helicopter as a reconnaissance vehicle, although the M551 Sheridan was intended to be the primary ground role system. Unfortunately, the Sheridan has proved to be a relative failure, due mainly to an over-ambitious

LAV-25

Type: Light armored vehicle.
Crew: 3.
Armament: M242 25mm Bushmaster automatic cannon; M240 7·62mm co-axial MG.
Armor: Steel, sufficient to withstand 7·62mm AP in front, 7·62mm elsewhere.
Dimensions: Length 21ft (6·4m); width 7ft 2½in (2·2m) height 8ft 2½in (2·5m).
Weights: Empty 19,850lb (9,004kg); combat loaded 27,559lb (12,501kg).
Engine: Detroit Diesel 6V-53T, 6-cylinder turbocharged diesel; 275hp at 2,800rpm.
Performance: Maximum road speed 63mph (101km/h); road range 485 miles (781km); swimming speed 6mph (9·65km/h); gradient 70 per cent; side slope 35 per cent.

In 1981-82 the US Army's Tank-Automotive Command (TACom) carried out a series of tests for a light armored vehicle (LAV) to be procured for the US Army and US Marine Corps. Four vehicles were tested: the British Alvis Scorpion-Stormer, the Swiss-designed but Canadian-produced MOWAG "Piranha", and the Cadillac-Gage V-150 and V-300. The Scorpion-Stormer

operational requirement which tried to put too much into too small a vehicle and also stretched technology to breaking point. The situation became so bad that the somewhat unsuitable M60 Main Battle Tank had to be pressed into service for a short period. The new reconnaissance vehicle— the M3—is now entering service, much to the relief of the cavalry. For non-European scenarios the Army is looking to the Light Armored Vehicle (LAV), its first wheeled combat vehicle since the Stag armored car of World War II. Unfortunately, like so many programs, the LAV has hit political snags in the Congress, even though the Marine Corps requirement has been approved.

Above: The Light Armored Vehicle (LAV) started life in Switzerland as the MOWAG "Piranha". In 1983 it won the competition for an LAV for the US Army and USMC.

Left: This side shot of the LAV clearly shows its low silhouette. The main gun is the M242 Bushmaster automatic cannon. All eight wheels are driven by the 275hp diesel engine. In 1983 the US Congress denied the Army the funds for purchasing LAV.

series is tracked; the remainder are wheeled. Both the Army and Marine Corps required these vehicles for employment with the Rapid Deployment Force (RDF), although the Army's original requirement was reduced from 2,315 to 680 in 1982, and is now totally in doubt. Indeed, in mid-1983 the Congress denied funds for Army procurement of the LAV because it was considered that the requirement had not been properly justified. This is not to say, however, that the Army will not get its LAV in the long run.

The US Army's basic requirement is for a Mobile Protected Gun-Near Term (MPG-N), which differs substantially from the LAV required by the USMC. The Army plans to equip its light divisions with two MPG battalions, each with 41 LAVs and 40 HMMWVs (Hummer), for reconnaissance, fire support, and anti-tank defense. These battalions appear—on paper, at least—to be too lightly equipped, even for the RDF.

M551 Sheridan

Type: Light tank.
Crew: 4.
Armament: One 152mm gun/missile launcher; one 7·62mm machine-gun co-axial with main armament; one 0·5in anti-aircraft machine-gun; four smoke dischargers on each side of turret.
Armor: Classified.
Dimensions: Length 20ft 8in (6·299m); width 9ft 3in (2·819m); height (overall) 9ft 8in (2·946m).
Weight: Combat 34,898lbs (15,830kg).
Ground pressure: 6·96lb/in² (0·49kg/cm²).
Engine: Detroit Diesel 6V53T six-cylinder diesel developing 300bhp at 2,800rpm.
Performance: Road speed 45mph (70km/h); water speed 3·6mph (5·8km/h); range 373 miles (600km); vertical obstacle 2ft 9in (0·838m); trench 8ft 4in (2·54m); gradient 60 per cent.
History: Entered service with United States Army in 1966 and still in service.

In August 1959 the United States Army established a requirement for a "new armored vehicle with increased capabilities over any other weapon in its own inventory and that of any adversary". The following year the Allison Division of General Motors was awarded a contract to design a vehicle called the Armored Reconnaissance Airborne Assault Vehicle (ARAAV) to meet the requirement. The first prototype, designated XM551, was completed in 1962, and this was followed by a further 11 prototypes. Late in 1965 a production contract was awarded to Allison, and the first production vehicles were completed in 1966, these being known as the M551 or Sheridan. Production was completed in 1970 after 1,700 vehicles had been built.

The hull of the Sheridan is of all-aluminum construction whilst the turret is of welded steel. The driver is seated at the front of the hull and the other three crew members are in the turret, with the loader on the left and the gunner and commander on the right. The engine and transmission are at the rear of the hull. The suspension is of the torsion-bar type and consists of five road wheels, with the drive sprocket at the rear and the idler at the front. There are no track-return rollers. The most interesting feature of the

Sheridan is its armament system. This consists of a 152mm gun/launcher which has an elevation of +19° and a depression of −8°, traverse being 360°. A 7·62mm machine-gun is mounted co-axially with the main armament, and there is a 0·5in Browning machine-gun on the commander's cupola. The latter cannot be aimed and fired from within the turret, and as a result of combat experience in Vietnam many vehicles have now been fitted with a shield for this weapon. The 152mm gun/launcher, later fitted to the M60A2 and MBT-70 tanks, can fire either a Shillelagh missile or a variety of conventional ammunition including HEAT-T-MP, WP and canister, all of them having a combustible cartridge case. The Shillelagh missile was developed by the United States Army Missile Command and the Philco-Ford Corporation, and has a maximum range of about 3,281 yards (3,000m). The missile is controlled by the gunner, who simply has to keep the cross-hairs of his sight on the target to ensure a hit; however, severe problems exist in "capturing" the missile, making it of little value at ranges under 1,300 yards (1,200m). The missile itself weighs 59lbs (26·7kg) and has a single-stage solid-propellant motor which has a burn time of 1·18 seconds. Once the missile leaves the gun/missile-launcher, four fins at the rear of the missile unfold and it is guided to the target by a two-way infra-red command link which eliminates the need for the gunner to estimate the lead and range of the target. A Sheridan normally carries ten missiles and 20 rounds of ammunition, but this mix can be adjusted as required. In addition, 1,000 rounds of 0·5in and 3,080 rounds of 7·62mm ammunition are carried. The Sheridan is provided with a flotation screen, and when erected this enables the vehicle to propel itself across rivers and streams by its tracks. Night-vision equipment is provided as is an NBC system.

The M551 has not been a success. Its development was long and expensive, and a further in-service product-improvement program has failed to bring it up to an acceptable standard. As a result, it has long since been replaced by the M60 in reconnaissance units in US Army Europe. It remains in service only with the tank battalions of 82nd Airborne Division (57 tanks); a number are used at the National Training Center, Fort Irwin, mainly as simulated Soviet vehicles.

Below: M551 Sheridan demonstrating its amphibious capability—an essential element for its reconnaissance role.

Below left: M551s show 152mm gun/launcher barrels. Combining the best aspects of gun and missile was fine only on paper.

Self-propelled Artillery

Since the end of World War II the US Army has led the increasingly rapid conversion from towed to self-propelled artillery. The M109 and M110 have become the standard weapons of most NATO armies and are reliable and effective,

M109A2

Type: Self-propelled howitzer.
Crew: 6.
Armament: One 155mm howitzer; one ·5in (12·7mm) Browning anti-aircraft machine-gun.
Armor: 20mm (0·79in) maximum, estimated.
Dimensions: Length (including armament) 21ft 8in (6·612m); length (hull) 20ft 6in (6·256m); width 10ft 10in (3·295m); height (including anti-aircraft machine-gun) 10ft 10in (3·295m).
Weight: Combat 55,000lb (24,948kg).
Ground Pressure: 10·95lb/in² (0·77kg/cm²).
Engine: Detroit Diesel Model 8V71T eight-cylinder turbocharged diesel developing 405bhp at 2,300rpm.
Performance: Road speed 35mph (56km/h); range 242 miles (390km); vertical obstacle 1ft 9in (0·533m); trench 6ft (1·828m); gradient 60 per cent.
History: Entered service with the United States Army in 1963. Also used by Austria, Belgium, Canada, Denmark, Germany, Great Britain, Ethiopia, Greece, Iran, Israel, Italy, Jordan, Kampuchea, Kuwait, Libya, Morocco, the Netherlands, Norway, Oman, Pakistan, Saudi Arabia, Spain, South Korea, Switzerland, Taiwan, Tunisia and Turkey. Still in production.

The first production models of the M109 were completed in 1962, and some 3,700 examples have now been built (of which about 1,800 are in US Army service), making the M109 the most widely used self-propelled howitzer in the world. It has a hull of all-welded aluminum construction, providing the crew with protection from small arms fire. The driver is seated at the front of the hull on the left, with the engine to his right. The other five crew members are the commander, gunner and three ammunition members, all located in the turret at the rear of the hull. There is a large door in the rear of the hull for ammunition resupply purposes. Hatches are also provided in the sides and rear of the turret. There are two hatches in the roof of the turret, the commander's hatch being on the right. A 0·5in (12·7mm) Browning machine-gun is mounted on this for anti-aircraft defense. The suspension is of the torsion-bar type and consists of seven road wheels, with the drive sprockets at the front and the idler at the rear, and there are no track-return rollers.

The 155mm howitzer has an elevation of +75° and a depression of −3°, and the turret can be traversed through 360°. Elevation and traverse are powered, with manual controls for emergency use. The weapon can fire a variety of ammunition, including HE, tactical nuclear, illuminating, smoke and chemical rounds. Rate of fire is four rounds per minute for three minutes, followed by one round per minute for the next hour. A total of 28 rounds of separate-loading ammunition is carried, as well as 500 rounds of machine-

although their range is not as good as that of comparable Soviet equipments. One major complication is that rates of fire are now so high that special arrangements are having to be made to ensure that the logistic system will be able to cope with the resupply requirement. Artillery has always been somewhat ineffective against armored vehicles—the major contemporary threat to the US Army in Europe—and great efforts are being made to overcome this. One attempt, the laser-guided Copperhead artillery shell, has failed to live up to expectations, but artillery shells are being developed which can deliver minelets, capable of attacking armored vehicles from above.

Above: The business end of the 155mm howitzer of the 2nd Field Artillery during a Reforger exercise in West Germany. Range of this basic M109 is 16,070 yards (14,700m); nuclear shells can be fired.

gun ammunition.

The second model to enter service was the M109A1, identical with the M109 apart from a much longer barrel, provided with a fume extractor as well as a muzzle-brake. The fume extractor removes propellant gases from the barrel after a round has been fired and thus prevents fumes from entering the fighting compartment. The M109A2 has an improved shell rammer and recoil mechanism, the M178 modified gun mount, and other more minor improvements. The M109A3 is the M109A1 fitted with the M178 gun mount. ▶

The M109 fires a round to a maximum range of 16,070 yards (14,700m); the M109A1 fires to a maximum range of 19,685 yards (18,000m). Rocket assisted projectiles (M549A1) increase the maximum range to 26,250 yards (24,000m). A new nuclear round (M785) is now under development: it is ballistically compatible with the M549A1 RAP and will utilize the same protective container as the M758 eight-inch round (*see M110A2 entry*).

The M109 can ford streams to a maximum depth of 6ft (1·828m). A special amphibious kit has been developed for the vehicle but this is not widely used. It consists of nine inflatable airbags, normally carried by a truck. Four of these are fitted to each side of the hull and the last to the front of the hull. The vehicle is then propelled in the water by its tracks at a maximum speed of 4mph (6·4km/h). The M109 is provided with infra-red driving lights and some vehicles also have an NBC system.

To keep the M109 supplied with ammunition in the field Bowen-McLaughlin-York have recently developed the M992 Field Artillery Ammunition Support Vehicle which is expected to enter production in the near future.

Right: M109A1 155mm SP howitzer fresh from the production line at the Cleveland Ordnance Plant, run by Cadillac Motor Car Division.

Below: An M109A2 of the US Army. This fine weapons system is in service with at least 28 armies and has proved a great success.

M110A2

M110, M110A1, M110A2

Type: Self-propelled howitzer.
Crew: 5 plus 8 (see text).
Armament: One 8in (203mm) howitzer.
Armor: 20mm (0·79in) maximum (estimated).
Dimensions: Length (including gun and spade in traveling position) 35ft 2½in (10·731m); length (hull) 18ft 9in (5·72m); width 10ft 4in (3·149m); height 10ft 4in (3·143m).
Weight: Combat 62,500lb (28,350kg).
Ground pressure: 10·80lb/in² (0·76kg/cm²).
Engine: Detroit Diesel Model 8V-7T eight-cylinder turbo-charged diesel developing 405bhp at 2,300rpm.
Performance: Road speed 34mph (54·7km/h); range 325 miles (523km); vertical obstacle 3ft 4in (1·016m); trench 7ft 9in (2·362m); gradient 60 per cent.
History: Original version, M110, entered service with the United States Army in 1963. Now used by Belgium, West Germany, Greece, Iran, Israel, Japan, Jordan, Saudi Arabia, South Korea, Netherlands, Pakistan, Spain, Turkey, United Kingdom and United States.

In 1956 the United States Army issued a requirement for a range of self-propelled artillery which would be air-transportable. The Pacific Car and Foundry Company of Washington were awarded the development contract and from 1958 built three different self-propelled weapons on the same chassis. These were the T235 (175mm gun), which became the

M107, the T236 (203mm howitzer), which became the M110, and the T245 (155mm gun), which was subsequently dropped from the range. These prototypes were powered by a petrol engine, but it was soon decided to replace this by a diesel engine as this could give the vehicles a much greater range of action. The M107 is no longer in service with the US Army; all have been rebuilt to M110A2 configuration. The M110A2 is also in production by Bowen-McLaughlin-York Company, and when present orders have been completed the US Army wil have a total inventory of over 1,000.

The hull is of all-welded-steel construction with the driver at the front on the left with the engine to his right. The gun is mounted towards the rear of the hull. The suspension is of the torsion-bar type and consists of five road wheels, with the fifth road wheel acting as the idler, the drive sprocket is at the front. Five crew are carried on the gun (driver, commander and three gun crew), the other eight crew members following in an M548 tracked vehicle (this is based on the M113 APC chassis), which also carries the ammunition, as only two ready rounds are carried on the M110 itself. The 203mm howitzer has an elevation of +65° and a depression of −2°, traverse being 30° left and 30° right. Elevation and traverse are both hydraulic, although there are manual controls for use in an emergency. The M110 fires an HE projectile to a maximum range of 26,575 yards (24,300m), and other types of projectile that can be fired include HE carrying 104 HE grenades, HE carrying 195 grenades, Agent GB or VX and tactical nuclear. A large hydraulically-operated spade is mounted at the rear of the hull and is lowered into position before the gun opens fire, and the suspension can also ▶

Below: M110A2 of the US Army. This version has the new M201 cannon which is 8ft (2·44m) longer than that mounted on the M110. The major shortcoming is the lack of a protective gun housing.

▶ be locked when the gun is fired to provide a more stable firing platform. The gun can officially fire one round per two minutes, but a well trained crew can fire one round per minute for short periods. As the projectile is very heavy, an hydraulic hoist is provided to position the projectile on the ramming tray; the round is then pushed into the breech hydraulically before the charge is pushed home, the breechlock closed and the weapon is then fired. The M110 can ford streams to a maximum depth of 3ft 6in (1·066m) but has no amphibious capability. Infra-red driving lights are fitted as standard but the type does not have an NBC system.

All M110s in US Army service, and in an increasing number of NATO countries as well, have been brought up to M110A2 configuration. The M110A1 has a new and longer barrel, while the M110A2 is identical to the M110A1 but has a double baffle muzzle brake. The M110A1 can fire up to charge eight while the M110A2 can fire up to charge nine. The M110A1/ M110A2 can fire all of the rounds of the M110 but in addition binary, high-explosive Rocket Assisted Projectile (M650), and the improved con-

Below: Loading the M110A2, improved version of the Army's heaviest cannon artillery weapon. It has conventional and nuclear capability.

ventional munition which contains 195 M42 grenades. The latter two have a maximum range, with charge nine, of 32,800 yards (30,000m).

The M110A2 also fires the M753 rocket-assisted tactical nuclear round, which entered production in FY 1981. The M753 will be available in two versions: the first as a normal nuclear round; the second as an "Enhanced Radiation" version. These nuclear rounds are packed in very sophisticated containers to prevent unauthorized use and are subject to very stringent controls. The ER rounds will not be deployed outside the USA except in an emergency.

One major shortcoming of the M110 design has always been its lack of protection for the gun crew: it is virtually the only modern self-propelled gun to suffer such a deficiency. The US Army plans to rectify this by fitting a Crew Ballistic Shelter (CBS), a high, square gun housing that will improve survivability against small arms and shell fragments by some 33 per cent and will also provide collective NBC protection.

One of the problems with heavy artillery of this type is keeping the guns supplied with sufficient ammunition. As noted above the weapon is supported by an M548 tracked vehicle, and this in turn is kept supplied by 5- or 10-ton trucks.

Towed Artillery

The requirement for increased crew protection and greater mobility has led to the virtual total replacement of towed artillery pieces in the European theater by self-propelled guns and howitzers. As a result, towed artillery has been "relegated" to less taxing environments with airborne forces and

M102

Type: Light howitzer.
Caliber: 105mm.
Crew: 8.
Weight: 3,298lb (1,496kg).
Length firing: 22ft (6·718m).
Length traveling: 17ft (5·182m).
Height firing: 4·29ft (1·308m).
Height traveling: 5·22ft (1·594m).
Width: 6·44ft (1·964m).
Ground clearance: 1·08ft (0·33m).
Elevation: −5° to +75°.
Traverse: 360°.
Range: 12,576 yards (11,500m), standard ammunition; 16,513 yards (15,100m) with RAP.

The 105mm M102 was developed at Rock Island Arsenal to replace the standard 105mm M101 howitzer in both airborne and airmobile divisions. The first prototype was completed in 1962 and the weapon entered service in 1966. It was widely used in Vietnam. Improvements over the M101 include a reduction in weight, longer range, and it can be quickly traversed through 360°. Both the M101 and M102 were to have been replaced by a

Below: The M102 has served for many years in 82nd Airborne Division, for which its light weight and compact dimensions, combined with good stability and all-round traverse made it an ideal weapon. All-up weight of 3,298lb (1,496kg) has been achieved by extensive use of aluminum.

the Rapid Deployment Force (RDF). Thus, towed equipments are still in production and under development, and there is, of course, still a lucrative export market. Like other Western armies, the US Army still finds it difficult to obtain as much range for its shells for a given caliber as do the Soviets, unless recourse is made to esoteric devices such as Rocket Assisted Projectiles (RAP). The M198, however, is a very promising weapon and should become the standard US Army towed howitzer, replacing both the current 105mm and 155mm weapons. Its performance characteristics, however, are in most cases little better than the Soviet D30 howitzer of 122mm caliber.

Above: An M102 in action under a somewhat sparsely scrimmed camouflage net. The gun is resting on a firing turntable; a roller at the rear of the trail enables the gun to be traversed quickly.

new 105mm howitzer called the XM204, but this was cancelled by Congress in 1977 owing to both tactical and technical problems.

The M102 is normally deployed in battalions of 18 guns (each of these having three batteries, each with 6 guns), and both the 82nd Airborne and 101st Airmobile/Air Assault Divisions each have three battalions of M102s, but these are now being replaced by the 155mm M198. It is normally towed by the M561 (6×6) Gama Goat vehicle or a 2½ ton 6×6 truck, and can be carried slung underneath a Boeing Chinook CH-47 helicopter.

When in the firing position the wheels are raised off the ground and the weapon rests on a turntable under the front of the carriage; a roller tire is mounted at the rear of the trail and this enables the weapon to be quickly traversed through 360° to be laid onto a new target. The M102 has an unusual bow shape box type trail which is of aluminum construction to reduce weight. Its breechblock is of the vertical sliding wedge type and its recoil system is of the hydropneumatic type. The barrel is not provided with a muzzle brake, although this was fitted to the prototype weapons. A wide range of ammunition can be fitted including high explosive, high explosive anti-tank, anti-personnel, illuminating, smoke, chemical, HEP-T, and leaflet. Ten rounds per minute can be fired for the first three minutes, and 3 rounds per minute in the sustained fire role.

M114A2

Type: Howitzer.
Caliber: 155mm.
Crew: 11.
Weight: 12,700lb (5,761kg).
Length traveling: 23·9ft (7·315mm).
Width traveling: 7·99ft (2·438m).
Height traveling: 5·9ft (1·8m).
Elevation: −2° to +63°.
Traverse: 25° right and 24° left.
Range: 21,106 yards (19,300m).

In 1939, Rock Island Arsenal started the development of a new 155mm towed howitzer to replace the 155mm M1918 howitzer which at that time was the standard 155mm howitzer of the US Army (this was basically a modified French 155mm weapon built in the United States). This new 155mm weapon was designated the M1 and first production weapons were completed in 1942. Production continued until after the end of the war by which time over 6,000 weapons had been built. After the war the M1 was redesignated the M114. The 4·5 inch M1 used the same carriage as the M114 but none of these remain in service today. A self-propelled model called the M41 was also built, but again, none of these remain in service with the US Army.

When the weapon is in the firing position, it is supported on its trails and a firing jack which is mounted under the carriage. When in the traveling position, the trails are locked together and attached to the prime mover, which is generally a 6x6 truck. The M114 can also be carried slung under a Boeing CH-47 Chinook helicopter.

Its recoil system is of the hydropneumatic variable type and its breech-block is of the stepped thread/interrupted screw type. The M114 can fire a variety of ammunition of separate loading type (eg, the projectile and a charge) including an HE round weighing 95lb (43kg), tactical nuclear,

Above: All Army M114A1s such as this are being converted to M114A2 standard by fitting a new cannon, developed as a result of a US Marine Corps initiative, which increases range by 32 per cent.

illuminating and chemical. Sustained rate of fire is one round per minute. It cannot however fire the new Rocket Assisted Round which has a longer range than the standard 155mm round.

The US Marine Corps developed a new tube for the M114 which has been adopted by the US Army as the M114A2. This tube is a ballistic match for that on the M109A2 (*qv*), and the M114A2 can thus fire all ammunition fired by its self-propelled counterpart. The M114A2 is used by general-support artillery units of the US Army Reserve and the National Guard.

Below: A fine action shot of an M114 showing how it is supported on two trail legs and a firing jack mounted underneath the carriage.

M198

Type: Towed howitzer.
Caliber: 155mm.
Crew: 10.
Weight: 15,795lb (7,165kg).
Length firing: 37ft 1in (11·302m).
Length traveling: 23ft 3in (7·086m).
Width firing: 28ft (8·534m).
Width traveling: 9ft 2in (2·79m).
Height firing (minimum): 5·91ft (1·803m).
Height traveling: 9·92ft (3·023m).
Ground clearance: 13in (0·33m).
Elevation: −4·2° to +72°.
Traverse: 22½° left and right; 360° with speed traverse.
Range: 32,808 yards (30,000m) with RAP; 24,060 yards (22,000m) with conventional round.

In the late 1960s, Rock Island Arsenal started work on a new 155mm howitzer to replace the M114, and this was given the development designation of the XM198. The first two prototypes were followed by eight further prototypes, and during extensive trials these weapons fired over 45,000 rounds of ammunition. The M198 is now in production at Rock Island; the Army has a requirement for 435 M198s while the Marine Corps requires 282. It has also been adopted by a number of other countries including Australia, India, Greece, Pakistan, Thailand and Saudi Arabia. The M198 is used by airborne, airmobile and infantry divisions. Other divisions will continue to use self-propelled artillery. The weapon will be developed in battalions of 18 guns, each battery having 6 weapons. The M198 is normally towed by a 6×6 5-ton truck or a tracked M548 cargo carrier, the latter being a member of the M113 family of tracked vehicles. It can also be carried under a Boeing CH-47 Chinook, but (and this is a most important drawback) its 5-ton prime mover cannot. A further problem is that the carriage is some 5in (127mm) too wide to fit into the Low-Attitude Parachute Extraction System (LAPES) rails in USAF C-130 aircraft.

When in the traveling position, the barrel is swung through 180° so that it rests over the trails. This reduces the overall length of the weapon. When in the firing position the trails are opened out and the suspension system is raised so that the weapon rests on a non-anchored firing platform. A hydraulic ram cylinder and a 24in (0·609m) diameter float mounted in the bottom carriage at the on-carriage traverse centerline provides for rapid shift of the carriage to ensure 360° traverse. This enables the weapon to be quickly laid onto a new target.

The weapon has a recoil system of the hydropneumatic type and the barrel is provided with a double baffle muzzle brake. The M198 uses separate loading ammunition (e.g. a projectile and a separate propelling charge) and can fire an HE round to a maximum range of 22,000m, or out to 30,000m with a Rocket Assisted Projectile. The latter is basically a conventional HE shell with a small rocket motor fitted at the rear to increase the range of the shell. The weapon will also be the primary user of the new Cannon Launched Guided Projectile (or Copperhead) round. Nuclear and Improved Conventional Munitions, as well as rounds at present used with the M114, can also be fired. It will also be able to fire the range of ammunition developed for the FH70. The latter is a joint development between Britain, Germany and Italy, and is now in production. Maximum rate of fire is four rounds per minute for the first three minutes, followed by two rounds per minute thereafter. A thermal warning device is provided so that the gun crew know when the barrel is becoming too hot.

Although a great improvement on its predecessors, the M198 has suffered from a number of problems. The desired range and accuracy requirements

Above: An M198 howitzer firing at its maximum elevation of 72°, a capability necessary to clear crests or to fire out of a jungle clearing. M198 will serve with artillery units in the US RDF.

have been achieved at the expense of mobility and size. Further, unit price has increased from an original estimate of $184,000 to $421,000—although the M198 is by no means the only weapon system to suffer such problems.

Aviation

The US Army possesses some 550 fixed-wing and 8,000 rotary-wing front-line aircraft; a larger air component than many air forces. These are, in the main, an integral part of the combat components of the Army, especially the Cavalry Brigades Air Attack. The helicopter force ranges in size

Beechcraft C-12
C-12, RC-12D, RU-21J

Type: Fixed-wing utility aircraft.
Engines: Two 850shp Pratt and Whitney of Canada PT6A-38 (C-12A) turboprops.
Dimensions: Overall length 43·75ft (13·34m); height 15ft (4·57m); wing span 54·5ft (16·61m); wing area 303ft² (28·15m²).
Weights: Gross weight (C-12) 12,500lb (5,670kg), (RC-12D) 14,000lb (6,350kg).
Performance: Cruising speed 242 knots (448km/h); range with full payload 1,681 nautical miles (3,115km); mission ceiling (C-12) 31,000ft (9,450m), (RC-12D) 27,000ft (8,230m).
Armament: Nil.
History: First flight (Super King Air 200) 27 October 1972; entered service (C-12A) July 1975.

Development: The C1-12, a military version of the Super King Air 200, is latest in a long line of small, fixed-wing utility aircraft used by the US Army. Its primary tasks are the transportation of priority cargo and passengers,

from the diminutive (but highly effective) Hughes OH-6 to the twin-rotor Boeing Vertol CH-47, and is being substantially improved by the UH-60 utility helicopter and the AH-64 attack helicopter. Large numbers of the older OH-58, UH-1, and AH-1 will, however, remain in service for many years to come. The size of the fixed-wing aircraft is limited to a specific weight by an inter-Service agreement with the USAF, but the Army still operates many OV-1 and RU-21/C-12 aircraft. For the future, the Army has been involved in the JVX program—a development of the Bell XV-15 technology—but like many previous joint-Service undertakings this has run into severe problems.

Above: Beechcraft RC-12D aircraft of the US Army, with an impressive array of antennas. A recent analysis of this aircraft suggests that its role is missile suppression in support of airborne operations.

Left: Beechcraft U-21 aircraft of the US Army, loading freight. The Army maintains a small fleet of U-21 and C-12 aircraft for flying urgent freight and passengers, but lost its heavier fixed-wing aircraft (such as the de Havilland Canada C-7) to the USAF in a politically inspired inter-Service transfer in 1967. The larger C-12 supplements the U-21 and is the basic version of the RC-12D. Some 98 C-12 transports are in service worldwide. With close monitoring by the USAF, larger Army aircraft will not be allowed.

and it has an all-weather day and night capability. Special equipment fits suit the basic airframe for intelligence gathering, airborne command post, or flying ambulance duties. The US Army has taken delivery of 60 C-12As, 14 C-12Cs (identical with the C-12A except for PT6A-41 engines), and 24 C-12Ds. The latter differs from the C-12C only in the fitting of a cargo door and wing-tip tanks.

The US Army has recently devoted a great deal of attention to airborne Electronic Warfare (EW) platforms. One such is the EH-60A Quick Fix (*see UH-60A entry*), but fixed-wing aircraft offer significant advantages over helicopters in this field. The most recent project is Guardrail V, which is designed to intercept and locate enemy ground transmissions in certain frequency bands. The original aircraft in Guardrail V was the RU-21H, the US Army version of the earlier Beech King Air, but under the Improved Guardrail V program, eight C-12s are being fitted out under the designation RC-12D, with antennas above and below the wing and ECM pods.

Bell AH-IS HueyCobra

Type: Attack helicopter.

Engine: 1,800shp Lycoming T53-L-703 turboshaft.

Dimensions: Main-rotor diameter 44ft (13·4m); overall length (rotors turning) 52ft 11½in (16·14m); length of fuselage 44ft 5in (13·54m); height 13ft 5½in (4·1m).

Weights: Empty 6,598lb (2,993kg); maximum 10,000lb (4,536kg).

Performance: Maximum speed (TOW configuration) 141mph (227km/h); max rate of climb (SL, rated power) 1,620ft (494m)/min; service ceiling (rated power) 12,200ft (3,719m); hovering ceiling in ground effect, same; range (max fuel, SL, 8% reserve) 315 miles (507km).

Armament: M65 system with nose telescope sight and crew helmet sights for cueing and guiding eight TOW missiles on outboard under-wing pylons; chin turret (to 100th AH-1S) M28 with 7·62mm Minigun and 40mm M129 grenade launcher with 300 bombs, (from No 101) GE Universal turret with 20mm M197 three-barrel gun (or alternative 30mm); also wide range of cluster/fuel-air explosive and other weapons or five types of rocket fired from 7 or 19-tube launchers.

History: First flight 7 September 1965; combat service June 1967 (TOW-Cobra January 1973, AH-1S March 1977).

Development: First flown in 1965 after only six months of development, the HueyCobra is a combat development of the UH-1 Iroquois family. It combines the dynamic parts—engine, transmission, and rotor system—of the original Huey with a new streamlined fuselage providing for a gunner in the front and pilot above and behind him and for a wide range of fixed and power-aimed armament systems. The first version was the US Army AH-1G, with 1,100hp T53 engine, of which 1,124 were delivered, including eight to the Spanish Navy for anti-ship strike and 38 as trainers to the US Marine Corps. The AH-1Q is an anti-armor version often called TOWCobra because it carries eight TOW missile pods as well as the appropriate sighting system. Latest versions are the -1Q, -1R, and -1S, with more power and new equipment.

The US Army plans to upgrade many earlier models to -1S standard, which, with 324 new production aircraft, will give a total fleet of 982. Several hundred are already in service. Thus, the HueyCobra, developed in just six months in 1965, will remain in front-line service with the US Army well into the 1990s and probably beyond the year 2000.

Above: Bell AH-1S at the moment of firing one of its TOW anti-tank guided missiles. The US Army plans to have a fleet of 982 AH-1s.

Above: The pilot's cockpit of an AH-1Q. The multiplicity of analog indicators clearly shows the 1960/70s origins of this ubiquitous aircraft, which will continue to serve the US Army into the next century.

Left: An AH-1S, showing one of the many weapons permutations possible. Note the nose sights and 7·62mm Minigun in the chin turret.

Bell OH-58C Kiowa

Type: Light observation helicopter/Army Helicopter Improvement Program (AHIP).

Engine: (OH-58A, TH-57A) one 317shp Allison T63-700 turboshaft, (OH-58C) 420shp T63-720.

Dimensions: Diameter of two-blade main rotor 35ft 4in (10·77m); length overall (rotors turning) 40ft 11¾in (12·49m); height 9ft 6½in (2·91m).

Weights: Empty (C) 1,585lb (719kg), (D) 2,825lb (1,281kg); maximum (C) 3,200lb (1,451kg).

Performance: Maximum speed 139mph (224km/h); service ceiling (C) 19,000ft (5,791m); range (SL, no weapons, 10% reserve) 299 miles (481km).

Armament: Usually none (see text).

History: First flight (OH-4A) 8 December 1962, (206A) 10 January 1966, (production OH-58C) 1978, (AHIP) 1983.

Development: The loser in the US Army Light Observation Helicopter contest of 1962, the 206 was marketed as the civil JetRanger, this family growing to encompass the more powerful 206B and more capacious 206L LongRanger. In 1968 the US Army re-opened the LOH competition, naming Bell now winner and buying 2,200 OH-58A Kiowas similar to the 206A but

with larger main rotor. Since 1976 Bell has been rebuilding 585 OH-58A Kiowas to OH-58C standard with uprated engine, flat-plate canopy to reduce glint, new instrument panel, improved avionics, and many minor improvements. Standard armament kit, not always fitted, is the M27 with a 7·62mm Minigun firing ahead.

In 1981 Bell was named winner of the AHIP (Army Helicopter Improvement Program) for a "near-term scout". The first of five prototype Model 406 AHIP machines flew in 1983. Features include a new rotor with four composite blades driven by a much more powerful T63-type (Model 250) engine, very comprehensive protection systems, and a mast-mounted ball with TV and FLIR (forward-looking infra-red), laser ranger/designator, inertial navigation, and one or two pairs of MLMS missiles.

The AHIP will serve in air cavalry, attack helicopter, and field artillery units. One of its main tasks will be target acquisition and laser designation for Hellfire missiles, Copperhead, and other US Army/USAF laser-guided munitions. The number of OH-58As and -58Cs to be converted to AHIP standard has yet to be decided, but it is hoped that the first 16 will be available in FY84.

Below: The Bell OH-58C Kiowa is a modified version of the earlier OH-58A with a more powerful engine, uprated transmission and an anti-glare flat-glass canopy. More minor improvements have also been fitted, like the infra-red suppressed exhaust stacks seen here.

Bell UH-1H Iroquois (Huey)

Type: Utility helicopter.

Engine: Originally, one Lycoming T53 free-turbine turboshaft rated at 600-640shp, later rising in stages to 825,930, 1,100 and 1,400shp; (212) 1,800shp P&WC PT6T-3 (T400) coupled turboshafts, flat-rated at 1,250shp and with 900shp immediately available from either following failure of the other.

Dimensions: Diameter of twin-blade main rotor (204, UH-1B, C) 44ft 0in (13·41m), (205,212) 48ft 0in (14·63m) (tracking tips, 48ft 2¼in, 14·69m); (214) 50ft 0in (15·24m); overall length (rotors turning) (early) 53ft 0in (16·15m), (virtually all modern versions) 57ft 3¼in (17·46m); height overall (modern, typical) 14ft 4¾in (4·39m).

Weights: Empty (XH-40) about 4,000lb (1,814kg), (typical 205) 4,667lb (2,110kg), (typical 212) 5,549lb (2,517kg); maximum loaded (XH-40) 5,800lb (2,631kg), (typical 205) 9,500lb (4,309kg), (212/UH-1N) 10,500lb (4,762kg).

Performance: Maximum speed (all) typically 127mph (204km/h); econ cruise speed, usually same; max range with useful payload, typically 248 miles (400km).

Armament: See text.

History: First flight (XH-40) 22 October 1956, (production UH-1) 1958, (205) August 1961, (212) 1969.

Development: Used by more air forces, and built in greater numbers, than any other military aircraft since World War II, the "Huey" family of helicopters grew from a single prototype, the XH-40, for the US Army. Over 20 years the gross weight has been almost multiplied by three, though the size has changed only slightly. Early versions seat eight to ten, carried the occasional machine-gun, and included the TH-1L Seawolf trainer for the US Navy. Prior to 1962 the Army/Navy designation was basically HU-1, which gave rise to the name Huey, though the (rarely used) official name is Iroquois. Since 1962 the basic designation has been UH-1 (utility helicopter type 1).

In August 1961 Bell flew the first Model 205 with many changes of which

Above: Some 3,500 Bell UH-1H are in US Army service; despite many new helicopters entering service the UH-1 will remain until after 2000.

the greatest was a longer fuselage giving room for up to 14 passengers or troops, or six litters (stretchers) and an attendant, or up to 3,880lb (1,759kg) of cargo. All versions have blind-flying instruments, night lighting, FM/VHF/UHF radios, IFF transponder, DF/VOR, powered controls, and searchlight. Options include a hook for a slung load, rescue hoist, and various fits of simple weapons or armor. Newest and most important of the Model 205 helicopters in US military service is the UH-1H, which remained in production until 1980. Ten have been converted as EH-1H Quick Fix EW (electronic-warfare) machines, but this role has been taken over by the more powerful EH-60A. Two were given augmented avionics and special equipment as UH-1V medevac transports.

Some 3,900 UH-1s are currently in US Army service; about 3,500 are the UH-1H model, which was introduced in 1967. Some 2,700 of the -1Hs are scheduled to remain in service beyond the year 2000 for a wide range of duties, and apart from fitting glassfiber composite blades they will be completely upgraded with over 220 new items or improvements including a radar-warning receiver, chaff/flare dispenser, IR jammer, exhaust IR suppressor, radar altimeter, DME, and secure communications even in NOE (nap of the Earth) flying.

Left: Troopers of 1st Cavalry (Airmobile) doing a "hoverjump" from a UH-1D during Operation Oregon (August 1967) in the Vietnam War.

Below: The Vietnam War saw an unprecedented advance in the use of the helicopter on the battlefield: UH-1H delivers troops at a LP.

Boeing Vertol
CH-47D Chinook

Type: Medium transport helicopter.
Engines: Two 3,750shp Lycoming T55-L-11A free-turbine turboshafts.
Dimensions: Diameter of main rotors 60ft (18·29m); length, rotors turning, 99ft (30·2m); length of fuselage 51ft (15.54m); height 18ft 7in (5·67m).
Weights: Empty 20,616lb (9,351kg); loaded (condition 1) 33,000lb (14,969kg); (overload condition II) 46,000lb (20,865kg).
Performance: Maximum speed (condition I) 189mph (304km/h); (II) 142mph (229km/h); initial climb (I) 2,880ft (878m)/min; (II) 1,320ft (402m)/min; service ceiling (I) 15,000ft (4,570m); (II) 8,000ft (2,440m); mission radius, cruising speed and payload (I) 115 miles (185km) at 158mph (254km/h) with 7,262lb (3,294kg); (II) 23 miles (37km) at 131mph (211km/h) with 23,212lb (10,528kg).
Armament: Normally none.
History: First flight (YCH-47A) 21 September 1961, (CH-47C) 14 October 1967, (D) 11 May 1979.

▶

Above: US Army troops wait to board a prototype CH-47D, the latest model of this versatile and extremely capable aircraft.

Left: An early model CH-47 delivers a water trailer to a forward position, its downdraught demolishing troops' "hootchies"!

Below: A CH-47C delivers an M102 105mm light howitzer, a load well within its capabilities. The -D model has three cargo hooks.

▶ **Development:** Development of the Vertol 114 began in 1956 to meet the need of the US Army for a turbine-engined all-weather cargo helicopter able to operate effectively in the most adverse conditions of altitude and temperature. Retaining the tandem-rotor configuration, the first YCH-47A flew on the power of two 2,200shp Lycoming T55 turboshaft engines and led directly to the production CH-47A. With an unobstructed cabin 7½ft (2·29m) wide, 6½ft (1·98m) high and over 30ft (9·2m) long, the Chinook proved a valuable vehicle, soon standardized as US Army medium helicopter and deployed all over the world. By 1972 more than 550 had served in Vietnam, mainly in the battlefield airlift of troops and weapons but also rescuing civilians (on one occasion 147 refugees and their belongings were carried to safety in one Chinook) and lifting back for salvage or repair 11,500 disabled aircraft valued at more than $3,000 million. The A model gave way to the CH-47B, with 2,850hp engines and numerous improvements. Since 1967 the standard basic version has been the CH-47C, with much greater power and increased internal fuel capacity. Most exports by BV are of this model, which in 1973 began to receive a crashworthy fuel system and integral spar inspection system.

In the late 1970s there was a resurgence of orders, and by 1981 they

Above: These two non-standard Chinooks were modified CH-47Bs with additional sensors fitted in the nose for night observation and attack trials. They have since been rebuilt to the CH-47D standard.

were nearing 1,000, with many new customers. Argentina's Type 308 is an Antarctic logistic/rescue machine with radar, duplex inertial navigation and range of 1,265 miles (2,036km). Canada's CH-147s have many advanced features, but the 33 Chinook HC.1 transports of the RAF are to an even later standard with 44 seats or 24 stretcher casualties, triple cargo hooks (front and rear, 20,000lb, 9,072kg, center at 28,000lb, 12,700kg), Decca TacNav, doppler and area navigation, new cockpit lighting, L-11E engines driving folding glass/carbon-fiber blades and amphibious capability in Sea State 3.

Development work on the RAF Chinook has led to the CH-47D for the US Army. The first 436 D models will be converted from older machines, but these will be followed by 91 new-builds, for a total inventory of 527. These feature 3,750shp L-712 long-life engines, 7,500shp transmission, redundant and uprated electrics, glassfiber blades, modular hydraulics, triple cargo hook, advanced light control system, new avionics, single-point fueling, survivability gear, and T62 APU.

Grumman OV-1 Mohawk

OV-1A to -1D, EV-1, JOV, RV

Type: (OV) multi-sensor tactical observation and reconnaissance; (EV) electronic warfare; (JOV) armed reconnaissance; (RV) electronic reconnaissance.

Engines: Two 1,005shp Lycoming T53-7 or -15 free-turbine turboprops; (OV-1D) two, 1,160shp T53-701.

Dimensions: Span (-1A, -C) 42ft (12·8m); (-1, -D) 48ft (14·63m); length 41ft (12·5m); (-1D with SLAR, 44ft 11in); height 12ft 8in (3·86m).

Weights: Empty (-1A) 9,937lb (4,507kg); (-1B) 11,067lb (5,020kg); (-1C) 10,400lb (4,717kg); (-1D) 12,054lb (5,467kg); maximum loaded (-1A) 15,031lb (6,818kg); (11B, C) 19,230lb (8,722kg); (-1D) 18,109lb (8,214kg).

Performance: Maximum speed (all) 297-310mph (480-500km/h); initial climb (-1A) 2,950ft (900m)/min; (-1B) 2,250ft (716m)/min; (-1C), 2,670ft (814m)/min; (-1D) 3,618ft (1,103m)/min; service ceiling (all) 28,800-31,000ft (8,534-9,449m); range with external fuel (-1A) 1,410 miles (2,270km); (-1B) 1,230 miles (1,980km); (-1C) 1,330 miles (2,140km); (-1D), 1,011 miles (1,627km).

Armament: Not normally fitted, but can include a wide variety of air-to-ground weapons including grenade launchers, Minigun pods and small guided missiles.

History: First flight (YOV-1A) 14 April, 1959; service delivery, February 1961; final delivery (new aircraft) December 1970.

Development: Representing a unique class of military aircraft, the OV-1 Mohawk is a specially designed battlefield surveillance machine with characteristics roughly midway between lightplanes and jet fighters. One of its requirements was to operate from rough forward airstrips and it has exceptional STOL (short takeoff and landing) qualities and good low-speed control with full-span slats and triple fans and rudders. Pilot and observer sit in side-by-side Martin Baker J5 seats and all versions have extremely good all-round view and very comprehensive navigation and communications equipment. All versions carry cameras and upward-firing flares for night photography. Most variants carry UAS-4 infra-red surveillance equipment and the -1B carries APS-94 SLAR (side-looking airborne radar) in a long pod under the right side of the fuselage, with automatic film processing giving, within seconds of exposure, a permanent film record of radar image on either side of the flight path. The -1D combined the functions of the two previous versions in being quickly convertible to either IR or SLAR missions. Underwing pylons can carry 150 US gal drop tanks,

Above: OV-1D with Sideways-Looking Airborne Radar (SLAR) and Infra-Red (IR) sensors monitors Mount St Helens eruption.

ECM (electronic countermeasures) pods, flare/chaff dispensers, or, in the JOV-1A such weapons as FFAR pods, 0.50in gun pods or 500lb (227kg) bombs—though a 1965 Department of Defense rule forbids the US Army to arm its fixed-wing aircraft! The EV-1 is the OV-1B converted to electronic surveillance with an ALQ-133 target locator system in centerline and tip pods. The RV-1C and -1D are conversions of the OV-1C and -1D for permanent use in the electronic reconnaissance role. Total production of all versions was 371, and since the mid-1970s the USA has maintained a continuing modernization programme involving (by 1983) 91 earlier models to OV-1D standard, and four to RV-1D, to maintain a force of 110 OV-1Ds and 36 RV-1Ds into the 1990s.

Below left: An OV-1D painted in overall "low-contrast" grey, which is not in reality as light as it appears from this photograph.

Below: An early model OV-1 coming in to land at a forward airstrip.

Hughes AH-64 Apache

Model 77, AH-64

Type: Armed helicopter.

Engines: Two 1,536shp General Electric T700-700 free-turbine turbo-shafts.

Dimensions: Diameter of four-blade main rotor 48ft 0in (14·63m); length overall (rotors turning) 57ft ½in (17·39m); length of fuselage 49ft 1½in (14·97m); height to top of hub 13ft 10in (4·22m).

Weights: Empty 10,268lb (4,657kg); maximum loaded 17,650lb (8,006kg).

Performance: Maximum speed (13,925lb/6,316kg) 192mph (309km/h); maximum cruising speed 182mph (293km/h); max vertical climb 2,880ft (878m)/min; max range on internal fuel 380 miles (611km); ferry range 1,121 miles (1,804km).

Armament: Four wing hardpoints can carry 16 Hellfire missiles or 76 rockets (or mix of these weapons); turret under fuselage (designed to collapse harmlessly upwards in crash landing) houses 30mm Chain Gun with 1,200 rounds of varied types of ammunition.

History: First flight (YAH-64) 30 September 1975; entry into service scheduled 1984.

Development: A generation later than the cancelled Lockheed AH-56A Cheyenne (the world's first dedicated armed escort and attack helicopter), the AH-64 was selected as the US Army's standard future attack helicopter in December 1976. This followed competitive evaluation with the rival Bell YAH-63, which had tricycle landing gear and the pilot seated in front ▶

Right: The AH-64 Apache is visually one of the least attractive of modern helicopters, but is also the most potent combat machine of all.

Below: A development aircraft showing its heavy armament and "black hole" engine exhausts to defeat heat-seeking missiles.

▶ of the co-pilot/gunner. The basic development contract also included the Chain Gun, a lightweight gun (in 30mm calibre in this application) with a rotating lockless bolt. In 1977 development began of the advanced avionics, electro-optics and weapon-control systems, progressively fitted to three more prototypes, followed by a further three—designated Total Systems Aircraft—flown by early 1980. The 56-month development ended in mid-1981 and limited production began at the end of that year. Total US Army requirement is for 572 machines, but actual procurement may be rather less, because of rapid cost escalation.

Hughes is responsible for the rotors and dynamic components, while Teledyne Ryan produces the bulk of the rest of the airframe (fuselage, wings, engine nacelles, avionic bays, canopy and tail unit). The entire structure is designed to withstand hits with any type of ammunition up to 23mm calibre. The main blades, for example, each have five stainless-steel spars, with structural glassfiber tube linings, a laminated stainless steel skin and composite rear section, all bonded together. The main sensors are PNVS (pilot's night vision system) and TADS (target acquisition and designation sight) jointly developed by Martin Marietta and Northrop.

Both crew members are equipped with the Honeywell IHADSS (integrated helmet and display sight system) and each can in emergency fly the helicopter and control its weapons. The helicopter's nose sight incorporates day/night FLIR (forward-looking infra-red) laser ranger/designator and laser tracker. The AH-64 carries an ordnance load of some 2,650lb (1,202kg), which can include up to 16 Hellfire anti-tank missiles, 76 2·75in (6·98cm) rockets, up to 1,200 rounds for its 30mm cannon, or lesser combinations of these.

Below: An AH-64 armed with 2·75in (7cm) rockets and Hellfire anti-tank missiles. Under the nose is a Hughes 30mm cannon.

Above: An AH-64 demonstrating its ability to carry a maximum of 16 Hellfire anti-tank missiles. Typical mission weight is 13,920lb (6,314kg).

Hughes OH-6A Cayuse

Type: Light observation helicopter.
Engine: One Allison turboshaft T63-5A flat-rated at 252·5shp.
Dimensions: Diameter of four-blade main rotor 26ft 4in (8·03m); length overall (rotors turning) 30ft 3¼in (9·24m); height overall 8ft 1½in (2·48m).
Weights: Empty 1,229lb (557kg), maximum loaded 2,700lb (1,225kg).
Performance: Max cruise at S/L 150mph (241km/h); typical range on normal fuel 380 miles (611km).
Armament: See text.
History: First flight (OH-6A) 27 February 1963.

Development: Original winner of the controversial LOH (Light Observation Helicopter) competition of the US Army in 1961, the OH-6A Cayuse is one of the most compact flying machines in history, relative to its capability. The standard machine carries two crew and four equipped troops, or up to 1,000lb (454kg) of electronics and weapons including the XM-27 gun or XM-75 grenade launcher plus a wide range of other infantry weapons. The US Army bought 1,413 and several hundred other military or para-military examples have been built by Hughes or its licensees. In 1982 Hughes was in production with, or offering, nine military helicopters all significantly uprated compared with the Cayuse, and bristling with advanced avionics, sensors, weapons and protective features, but the only sale to the US

Sikorsky CH-54A Tarhe

Type: Crane helicopter.
Engines: (CH-54A) two 4,500shp Pratt & Whitney T73-1 turboshafts, (CH-54B) two 4,800shp T73-700.
Dimensions: Diameter of six-blade main rotor 72ft 0in (21·95m); length overall (rotors turning) 88ft 6in (26·97m); height overall 18ft 7in (5·67m).
Weights: Empty (A) 19,234lb (8,724kg); maximum loaded (A) 42,000lb (19,050kg), (B) 47,000lb (21,318kg).
Performance: Maximum cruise 105mph (169km/h); hovering ceiling out of ground effect 6,900ft (2,100m); range with max fuel and 10 per cent reserve (typical) 230 miles (370km).
Armament: Normally none.
History: First flight (S-64) 9 May 1962; service delivery (CH-54A) late 1964, (B) late 1969.

Development: Developed from the first large US Army helicopter, the S-56, via the piston-engined S-60, the S-64 is an efficient weight-lifter which in Vietnam carried loads weighing up to 20,000lb (9,072kg). The CH-54A Tarhes used in that campaign retrieved more than 380 shot-down aircraft, saving an estimated $210 million, and carried special vans housing up to 87 combat-equipped troops. The improved CH-54B, distinguished externally by twin main wheels, has lifted loads up to 40,780lb (18,497kg) and reached a height of 36,122ft (11,010m). There is no fuselage, just a structural beam joining the tail rotor to the cockpit in which seats are provided for three pilots, one facing to the rear for maneuvering with loads. The dynamic components (rotor, gearboxes, shafting) were used as the basis for those of the S-65. With cancellation of the HLH (Heavy-Lift Helicopter) the S-64 remains the only large crane helicopter in the West. A total of just over 100 was built, of which the US Army took delivery of 89; 72 of these currently survive.

By 1983 the CH-54 could be outperformed by the CH-47D and had been phased out of regular Army service. It remains in service with aviation units of the Army National Guard.

Above: Despite losing to Bell Kiowa in the AHIP competition, the OH-6D as an OH-6A Cayuse rebuild remains an attractive possibility.

military has been USA funding of a single research Notar (NO TAil Rotor) helicopter modified from an OH-6A.

Virtually all OH-6As in the US Army inventory are now with National Guard or Army Reserve units.

Above: The CH-54 has for many years been the only large crane helicopter in the Army, but is now only in service with the National Guard.

Sikorsky UH-60A Black Hawk

UH-60A, EH-60A

Type: (UH) combat assault transport, (EH) electronic warfare and target acquisition.

Engines: (UH, EH) two 1,560shp General Electric T700-700 free-turbine turboshafts.

Dimensions: Diameter of four-blade rotor 53ft 8in (16·36m); length overall (rotors turning) 64ft 10in (19·76m); length (rotors/tail folded) 41ft 4in (12·6m); height overall 16ft 10in (5·13m).

Weights: Empty 10,624lb (4,819kg); maximum loaded 20,250lb (9,185kg) (normal mission weight 16,260lb, 7,375kg).

Performance: Maximum speed, 184mph (296km/h); cruising speed 167mph (269km/h); range at max wt, 30 min reserves, 373 miles (600km).

Armament: (UH) provision for two M60 LMGs firing from side of cabin, plus chaff/flare dispensers; (EH) electronic only.

History: First flight (YUH) 17 October 1974, (production UH) October 1978, service delivery (UH) June 1979.

Development: The UH-60 was picked in December 1976 after four years of competition with Boeing Vertol for a UTTAS (utility tactical transport aircraft system) for the US Army. Designed to carry a squad of 11 equipped troops and a crew of three, the Black Hawk can have eight troop seats replaced by four litters (stretchers), and an 8,000lb (3,628kg) cargo load can be slung externally. The titanium/glassfibre/Nomex honeycomb rotor is electrically de-iced, as are the pilot windscreens, and equipment includes comprehensive navaids, communications and radar warning. Deliveries to the 101st Airborne Division took place in 1979-81, followed by a further ▶

Right: A UH-60A Black Hawk is off-loaded from a C-5 at Cairo West airport after flying in from the USA on a RDF exercise.

Below: In their true element a group of UH-60s collecting troops from an ad hoc landing zone in scrubland, during an exercise in the USA.

block of 100 to the 82nd Division in 1981. It is now also in service with 9th and 24th Infantry Divisions in CONUS, and with US Army Europe. Because it is much more capable than the UH-1 it is replacing the older machine in a ratio of 15:23 in combat support companies and 7:8 in air cavalry units. The current aim is to field a total of 1,107 UH-60As at a cost of $6·58 billion (of which R&D accounts for $481 million).

The EH-60A is an ECM (electronic countermeasures) version with Quick Fix II (as used in the Bell EH-1H) radar warning augmentation, chaff/flare dispenser, and infra-red jammer. The EH-60B SOTAS (stand-off target acquisition system) was to have been a dedicated platform for detecting and classifying moving battlefield targets under all weather conditions, with a data terminal in the cabin fed from a large rotating surveillance radar aerial under the fuselage (the main wheels retracting to avoid it), but it was canceled in 1981.

Right: One of the YUH-60 prototypes during trials with a squad of 11 equipped troops. The Army has ordered 1,107 of these machines.

Below: The ability to allow four soldiers to descend by rope at the same time greatly reduces the vulnerable period in the hover.

Remotely Piloted Vehicles (RPV)

Following the great strides made in RPV technology during the Vietnam War (mainly in an Air Force context) and the recent Israeli successes, the US Army is now heavily involved in RPV development. The program, currently funded at some $395 million over the Fiscal Years 1982-85, is

Aquila (Army RPV)

Type: Remotely piloted vehicle.
Engine: One McCulloch MC101 M/C, 10hp.
Dimensions: Wingspan 12·33ft (3·76m); length 5·41ft (1·65m).
Weights: Maximum takeoff 119·1lb (54.4kg); payload 35·93lb (16.3kg).
Performance: Maximum speed 140mph (222km/h); maximum endurance 3 hours; ceiling 11,800ft (3,600m) plus.
Armament: None.
History: First flight December 1975. *(Specifications relate to Aquila.)*

Most modern armies are now faced with a problem of possessing artillery systems that far outperform the current target acquisition means. These new artillery systems have much increased range and markedly shorter response times; thus, the ground commander needs long-range, responsive reconnaissance systems transmitting data in real or near-real time. This ▶

Below and right: Launch and recovery of the Army's RPV test vehicle, based on the Lockheed Aquila. Control is with the ground commander throughout. The RPV is difficult to detect and hit and can transmit or record battlefield images and information. It is unlikely that service operation will commence before 1988.

intended to produce a system which will improve the Army's ability to locate targets, adjust artillery fire, and designate targets for laser-guided weapons. Such RPVs are very difficult to detect and, unlike manned aircraft, a hit does not involve the loss of a valuable, highly trained pilot. Further, they offer to ground commanders—always slightly suspicious of aircraft not under their direct command—an airborne reconnaissance system under their total control. Unfortunately, even though the RPV looks like a straight and simple military adaptation of a model airplane, the program has proved to be very expensive and also far more complex than had originally been anticipated.

▶ almost inevitably means a system under his own direct control. The Israelis have demonstrated the effectiveness of such systems with their Scout Mini-RPV. Another requirement is for an airborne laser designator system cheaper and tougher than a fixed-wing aircraft or helicopter.

The US Army's first venture into this field was the XMQM-105 Lockheed Aquila Mini-RPV, which was basically a limited "technology demonstrator" program. Four launch/control stations were produced, together with 30 Mini-RPVs. The payload comprises a stabilized TV camera and a laser.

Experience gained with the Aquila has been fed into the Army RPV program which has been under development since 1979. The requirement is for 72 launch/control stations and 780 RPVs, but current contracts cover only three ground units and 22 RPVs. Present estimates are that the total system costs will be in the region of $1·6 billion. There have been considerable problems, mainly arising from the requirement for a very small airframe to avoid detection by the enemy. As a result, it has proved very difficult to fit in all the components: TV, laser, data down-link, up-link receiver, and vehicle control systems.

The present RPV, made of Kevlar, is some 6ft (1·83m) long, has a wingspan of just under 13ft (3·96m), and weighs some 220lb (99·8kg). It is powered by a 24hp twin-cylinder engine driving a pusher propeller, giving a speed range of 56-113mph (90-182km/h). Endurance is some three hours. The RPV has proved very difficult to detect and, when found, has escaped damage even when under heavy fire.

Despite the apparent simplicity of the requirement the program is proving to be both lengthy and very expensive. The US Army is currently also looking at the Canadair CL-289 re-usable drone, a development of the CL-89 which has been used with great success by various other NATO armies since 1972.

Above: Canadair's CL-289 re-usable drone, which has been the subject of US Army evaluation, including troop trials.

Below: Difficulties with Aquila include keeping the guidance, optical and transmission systems within stringent size and weight restrictions. There is a 43lb (19·5kg) unit under the nose, with surveillance camera, target tracker and laser designator/rangefinder.

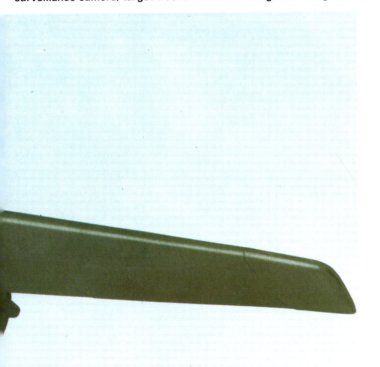

Theater Rockets and Missiles

Nowhere is American technological excellence more clearly seen than in the US Army's rocket and missile systems. The Pershing II system has now become one of the few Army weapons to have a truly strategic significance, for this new missile possesses a range sufficient to reach well into

Lance, MGM-52C

Type: Battlefield support missile.
Dimensions: Length 20ft 3in (6·17m); body diameter 22in (56cm).
Launch weight: 2,833 to 3,367lb (1,285-1,527kg) depending on warhead.
Propulsion: Rocketdyne P8E-9 storable-liquid two-part motor with infinitely throttleable sustainer portion.
Guidance: Simplified inertial.
Range: 45 to 75 miles (70-1120km) depending on warhead.
Flight speed: Mach 3.
Warhead: M234 nuclear 468lb (212kg, 10kT), W-70-4 ER/RB (neutron) or Honeywell M251, 1,000lb (454kg) HE cluster.

In service since 1972, this neat rocket replaced the earlier Honest John rocket and Sergeant ballistic missile, with very great gains in reduced system weight, cost and bulk and increases in accuracy and mobility. Usual vehicle is the M752 (M113 family) amphibious tracked launcher, with the M688 carrying two extra missiles and a loading hoist. For air-dropped operations a lightweight towed launcher can be used. In-flight guidance accuracy, with the precisely controlled sustainer and spin-stabilization, is already highly satisfactory, but a future missile could have DME (Distance Measuring Equipment) command guidance. The US Army has eight battalions, six of which are deployed in Europe with six launchers each; the two remaining

Below: US Army soldiers transferring a Lance missile from the loader-transporter vehicle (on the left) to the launcher vehicle. This very compact missile can carry nuclear, neutron, or high-explosive warheads.

the western military districts of the Soviet Union. In addition, its warhead is capable of attacking buried headquarters. Consequently, the fielding of Pershing II has become a major political issue, especially in Western Europe, as well as a bargaining counter in arms limitation talks. The most important rocket system in NATO's armies will soon be the Multiple Launcher Rocket System (MLRS), which will almost certainly become a standard NATO weapons system. Capable of high rates of fire, the MLRS is specifically intended to break up massed Warsaw Pact armor attacks. Unfortunately, like the latest self-propelled artillery, it is likely to impose severe strains on the resupply system.

Above: A Lance launch: flames and white smoke come from the rocket motor; black smoke from the front end comes from the spin motors. The Warsaw Pact has a whole series of battlefield missiles; the West has only two—US Lance and French Pluton.

battalions are at Fort Sill, Okla. Lance production lasted from 1971 to 1980, during which time 2,133 missiles were built.

Lance is the most powerful long-range missile currently under the direct control of the tactical ground commander. Its importance lies in its potential for breaking up Warsaw Pact second and third echelon forces before they can be committed. A successor in this vital mission is under development as the Corps Support Weapon System (CSWS). This is intended to carry an even wider variety of payloads over ranges up to 124 miles (200km), using simpler support equipment and requiring fewer men. Possible warheads include tactical nuclear, chemical, terminally-guided sub-munitions, and scatterable mines.

MLRS

Type: Multiple-launch rocket system.
Dimensions: (Rocket) length 13ft (3·96m); diameter 8·94in (227mm).
Launch weight: (Rocket) 600lb (272kg).
Propulsion: Atlantic Research solid rocket motor.
Range: Over 18·6 miles (30km).
Flight speed: Just supersonic.
Warhead: Dispenses payload of sub-munitions, initially 644 standard M42 bomblets.

Known from 1972 until 1979 as the GSRS (General Support Rocket System), the MLRS (Multiple Launch Rocket System) entered service with 1st Infantry Division (Mechanized) at Fort Riley, Kansas, in 1983. It has the same battlefield mobility as armored formations, being carried on a tracked vehicle which carries a trainable and elevating launcher; this can be rapidly loaded with two six-round containers without the crew of three leaving their cab. Each box houses six preloaded tubes with a 10-year shelf life. The crew can ripple-fire from two to 12 rounds in less than one minute, the fire control re-aiming after each shot. The rocket is highly accurate and is intended to carry any of three types of submunition, M42 shaped-charge grenade-size, scatterable anti-armor mines, or guided sub-missiles. In the ▶

Below: An MLRS rocket at the moment of launch. The rocket is 13ft (3·96m) long and 9in (230mm) in diameter; it weighs 600lb (272kg).

Above: MLRS vehicle with launch platform in the traveling position. Note the two rocket containers, each with six pre-loaded tubes.

▶ future a binary chemical warhead may also be developed. Each launcher load of 12 missiles is said to "place almost 8,000 submunitions in an area the size of four (US) football fields". The first production system was delivered to the Army in early 1982, by which time $317 million had been voted for the first 112 vehicles and 6,210 rockets. Production is intended to rise to 5,000 rounds per month, in a program costing an estimated $4·2 billion.

The carrying vehicle is designated a Self-Propelled Launcher Loader (SPLL) and is based on the M2 IFV (*qv*). The SPLL weighs some 50,000lb (22,680kg) fully loaded and is air portable in a C-141 Starlifter. It can travel at 40mph (64km/h) and can ford a depth of 40in (1·02m), but is not amphibious.

One of the major problems with high rate-of-fire rocket systems is that

Above: MLRS ready to fire. The tracked, self-propelled launcher vehicle is derived from the M2/M3 IFV/CFV, and has the same cross-country capability.

of resupply, and MLRS is no exception. Each battery of nine launchers will have its own ammunition platoon of 18 resupply vehicles and trailers, and there will be many more farther back in the logistic system.

In mechanized and armored divisions there will be one MLRS battery in the general support battalion (with two batteries of M110A2), while light divisions will have an independent battery. There will be an MLRS battalion of three batteries with each corps.

The MLRS is also the subject of a major NATO program involving France, Italy, the Federal Republic of Germany, and the United Kingdom.

Pershing, MGM-31

Type: Battlefield support missile.
Dimensions: Length 34ft 6in (10·51m); body diameter 40in (1·01m); fin span about 80in (2·02m).
Launch weight: About 10,150lb (4,600kg).
Propulsion: Two Thiokol solid motors in tandem, first stage XM105, second stage XM106.
Guidance: Army-developed inertial made by Eclipse-Pioneer (Bendix).
Range: 100 to 460 miles (160-740km).
Flight speed: Mach 8 at burnout.
Warhead: Nuclear, usually W-50 of approximately 400kT.

Originally deployed in 1962 on XM474 tracked vehicles as Pershing 1, the standard US Army long-range missile system has now been modified to 1a standard, carried on four vehicles based on the M656 five-ton truck. All are transportable in a C-130. In 1976 the three battalions with the US 7th Army in Europe were updated with the ARS (Azimuth Reference System) allowing them quickly to use unsurveyed launch sites, and the SLA (Sequential Launch Adapter) allowing one launch control center easily to fire three missiles. To replenish inventory losses caused by practice firings, 66 additional Pershing 1a missiles were manufactured in 1978-80.

Deployment of Pershing 1a in mid-1983 totaled 108 launchers with US Army Europe and 72 with West German forces (these latter being operated by the Luftwaffe, not the Army). The US intends to replace its Pershing 1as with Pershing IIs on a one-for-one basis, but the intentions of the West German government are not yet known. ▶

Right and below: Pershing II prototype is launched during the test program. This missile, although designated a battlefield support weapon, has a range which takes it well beyond the combat zone.

Pershing II has been studied since 1969 and has been in full development since 1974. It mates the existing vehicle with Goodyear Radag (Radar area-correlation guidance) in the new nose of the missile. As the forebody plunges down towards its target the small active radar scans the ground at 120rpm and correlates the returns with stored target imagery. The terminal guidance corrects the trajectory by means of new delta control surfaces, giving c.e.p. expected to be within 120ft (36m). As a result a lighter and less-destructive warhead (reported to be based on the B61 bomb of some 15kT) can be used, which extends maximum range. The Pershing II is fitted with an "earth-penetrator" device which enables the nuclear warhead to "burrow" deep underground before exploding. This is clearly intended for use against buried facilities such as headquarters and communications centers.

Development of Pershing II was envisaged as being relatively simple and cheap, but it has, in the event, proved both complicated and expensive. One problem has been with the rocket motors, which are entirely new to obtain the greatly increased range. A further complication was the sudden

elevation of the Pershing II program into a major international issue, with the fielding of the missiles becoming a test of US determination. The problems were further compounded by repeated failures in the test program, but the final test was a success and full production has gone ahead. First fielding will take place in December 1984 and all 108 are due to be deployed by December 1985.

The reason for the furore over Pershing II stems from its quite exceptional accuracy. The "hard-target kill potential" of a nuclear warhead is derived from the formula: $(\text{Raw Yield})^{2/3} \div (\text{c.e.p.})^2$. This means that the effect can be increased by two methods. In the first, the raw yield is increased, but this not only leads to a larger warhead, and thus a larger missile, but also the rate of increase in effect decreases as the raw yield is increased, ie, there is a law of diminishing returns. The other method of achieving a greater effect is to increase the accuracy (ie, decrease the c.e.p.), and as the effect increases by the square of the c.e.p. this is far more efficacious. Hence, the c.e.p. of 120ft (36m) has led to a warhead of much less raw yield, but very much greater effect than that fitted to the Pershing 1a.

Left: A Pershing II battlefield support missile ready for launch from its mobile platform. The new re-entry vehicle has four triangular fins and contains a 15kT nuclear warhead, with an exceptional degree of accuracy—the circular error probable (c.e.p.) is a mere 120ft (36m).

Below: A West German Luftwaffe crewman raising a Pershing 1a missile to the vertical in preparation for a launch simulation. There are now 108 Pershing 1a in Western Europe with US forces and a further 72 with the Luftwaffe. All US missiles will be replaced by the Pershing II by the end of 1985.

Mortars

Mortars are known in most armies as "the battalion commander's artillery", since they are the major fire support asset under his direct command. Mortars provide a very effective means of bringing heavy fire to bear both speedily and accurately, while their light weight and simplicity of operation make them ideal weapons for the infantry. Unlike

M29A1

Type: Mortar.
Caliber: 81mm.
Weight of barrel: 27·99lb (12·7kg).
Weight of baseplate: 24·91lb (11·3kg).
Weight of bipod: 40lb (18·15kg).
Total weight with sight: 115lb (52·2kg).
Elevation: +40° to +85°.
Traverse: 4° left and 4° right.
Maximum range: 5,140 yards (4,700km).
Rate of fire: 30rpm for 1 minute; 4-12rpm sustained.

In service with US Army and some Allied countries, the 81mm M29 mortar is the standard medium mortar of the US Army and is in service in two basic models, infantry and self-propelled. The standard infantry model can be disassembled into three components, each of which can be carried by one man—baseplate, barrel, mount and sight. The exterior of the barrel is helically grooved both to reduce weight and to dissipate heat when a high rate of fire is being achieved.

The mortar is also mounted in the rear of a modified member of the M113 APC family called the M125A1. In this vehicle the mortar is mounted on a turntable and this enables it to be traversed quickly through 360° to be laid onto a new target. A total of 114 81mm mortar bombs are carried in the vehicle.

The mortar can fire a variety of mortar bombs including HE (the M374 bomb has a maximum range of 5,025 yards (4,595m)), white phosphorus (the M375 bomb has a maximum range of 5,180 yards (4,737m)) and illuminating (the M301 bomb has a maximum range of 3,444 yards (3,150m)). The 81mm M29 has been replaced in certain units by the new M224 60mm Lightweight Company Mortar.

M224

Type: Lightweight company mortar.
Caliber: 60mm.
Total weight: 46lb (20·9kg); (hand-held with M8 baseplate) 17lb (7·7kg).
Maximum range: 3,828 yards (3,500m).

During the Vietnam campaign, it was found that the standard 81mm M29 mortar was too heavy for the infantry to transport in rough terrain, even when disassembled into its three main components. In its place the old 60mm M19 mortar was used, but this had a short range. The M224 has been developed to replace the 81mm M29 mortar in non-mechanized

the Soviet Army, however, the US Army has done away with the larger caliber mortars and when the M252 81mm replaces the 4·2in (106mm) in a few years time it will be the largest in US service. This mortar is of British design (the ML L16, with a Canadian-designed baseplate of forged aluminum and the Canadian C2 sight) and was very successfully combat tested in the British campaign in the Falklands in 1982. Its total weight is some 78lb (35·4kg) and it can be broken down into three man-portable loads of about equal weight. Technology is unlikely to produce any major breakthroughs in mortars, although work on the ammunition has led to significant increases in range.

infantry, airmobile and airborne units at company level, and is also issued to the US Marine Corps. The weapon comprises a lightweight finned barrel, sight, M7 baseplate and bipod, although if required it can also be used with the lightweight M8 baseplate, in which case it is hand-held. The complete mortar weighs only 46lb (20·9kg) compared to the 81mm mortar which weighs 115 (52kg). The M224 fires an HE bomb which provides a substantial portion of the lethality of the 81mm mortar with a waterproof "horseshoe" snap-off, propellant increments, and the M734 multi-option fuze. This new fuze is set by hand and gives delayed detonation, impact, near-surface burst (0-3ft, 0-0·9m), or proximity burst (3-13ft, 0·9-3·96m).

The mortar can be used in conjunction with the AN/GVS-5 hand held laser rangefinder, this can range up to 10,936 yards (10,000m) to an accuracy of ±10·936 yards (±10m). This enables the mortar to engage a direct-fire target without firing a ranging bomb first. The M224 fires a variety of mortar bombs to a maximum range of 3,828 yards (3,500m) and is currently in production at Watervliet Arsenal. The Army has ordered 1,590 of these mortars while the Marine Corps has ordered 698.

Below: The thirty-year-old M29 mortar is gradually being replaced by the M224 60mm mortar in dismounted infantry units.

Air Defense Weapons

The full scale and severity of the potential threat by the Warsaw Pact air forces to NATO ground forces is only now beginning to be fully appreciated. The US Army is trying to cope with this threat through a "layered" approach. At

Chaparral, M48

Type: Forward area air-defense missile system.
Dimensions: Length 114·5in (2·91m); body diameter 5·0in (12·7cm); span 25in (64cm).
Launch weight: 185lb (84kg).
Propulsion: Rocketdyne Mk 36 Mod 5 single-stage solid motor.
Guidance: Initial optical aiming, IR homing to target heat emitter.
Maximum range: About 5,250 yards (4,800m).
Maximum effective altitude: About 8,200ft (2,500m).
Flight speed: About Mach 2·5.
Warhead: (MIM-72C missile) 28lb (12·7kg) continuous rod HE.

When the purpose-designed Mauler missile was abandoned this weapon was substituted as a makeshift stop-gap, the missile being the original Sidewinder 1C modified for ground launch. A fire unit has four missiles on a manually tracked launcher, carried on an M730 (modified M548) tracked vehicle, with a further eight rounds on board ready to be loaded by hand.

Chaparral is widely used by the Army and Marine Corps, usually with an equal number of Vulcan air-defense gun systems. The missile now in production is MIM-72C, which not only carries a better warhead than the earlier version, but also has improved DAW-1 all-aspect guidance and the Harry Diamond Labs M-817 proximity fuze.

the lower end is the hand-held missile system, such as Stinger and Redeye. The next level was to have been the Euromissile Roland on a self-propelled launcher, but this has been reduced to a single battalion's worth mounted on a wheeled chassis, a humiliating end to a once proudly flaunted example of the "two-way street". At the divisional level there is a mix of the Sergeant York and Patriot systems, illustrating the still unresolved argument between the gun and missile lobbies. The US Army also operates the Improved Hawk and Nike Hercules missile systems, and at the very upper end of the spectrum will be responsible for any ballistic missile defense system which the USA may deploy.

Though totally inadequate, Chaparral is having to remain the USA's forward-area low-altitude SAM system for at least the next decade, instead of being replaced by Roland (*qv*) as originally planned. As a result, the US Army has begun an improvement program that includes fitting the launchers with a thermal-imaging (TI) sight to give the system a night and (albeit limited) bad-weather capability. A smokeless motor to reduce the battlefield signature is also being fitted.

The Chaparral system is now likely to have to remain in service until the mid-1990s.

Above and left: Chaparral fires four ready rounds (with eight reloads) of MIM-72C missiles. The gunner acquires targets visually or is cued by AN/MPQ-49 forward-area alerting radar, and tracks them optically until the missile's heat-seeking guidance takes over. The Army is having to make expensive modifications to maintain Chaparral's effectiveness, including retrofitting its launchers with FLIR to permit night and (some) bad-weather operations (since it would operate mostly in central Europe), and an improved guidance system with better resistance to aircraft infrared ECM.

Improved Hawk, MIM-23B

Type: Air-defense missile.
Dimensions: Length 16ft 6in (5·03m); body diameter 14in (360mm); span 48·85in (1,190mm).
Launch weight: 1,383lb (627·3kg).
Propulsion: Aerojet M112 boost/sustain solid rocket motor.
Guidance: CW radar SARH.
Range: 25 miles (40km).
Flight speed: Mach 2·5.
Warhead: HE blast/frag. 165lb (74·8kg).

Hawk (Homing All-the-Way Killer) was the world's first missile with CW guidance. When developed in the 1950s it looked a good system, but by modern standards it is cumbersome, each battery having a pulse acquisition radar, a CW illuminating radar, a range-only radar, two illuminator radars, battery control center, six three-missile launchers and a tracked loader, the whole weighing many tons. An SP version has ground-support items on wheels and towed by tracked launchers or loaders. Hawk became operational in August 1960 and is deployed widely throughout the Army and Marine Corps and 17 other nations.

Improved Hawk (MIM-23B) has a better guidance system, larger warhead, improved motor and semi-automatic ground systems ("certified rounds" are loaded in launchers without the need for further attention). Further development is attempting to improve CW radar reliability and improve pulse-acquisition speed by allowing automated threat-ordering of all targets that could be of importance.

It was originally intended that Improved Hawk would be replaced by Patriot by about 1987, but this changeover has now been postponed, probably until the early 1990s.

Nike Hercules, MIM-14B

Type: Large surface to air missile system for fixed emplacement.
Dimensions: Length 500in (41ft 8in, 1,270cm); body diameter 34·6in (88cm); span 105in (266cm).
Launch weight: 10,712lb (4,858kg).
Propulsion: Tandem boost motor, quad cluster with solid propellant; sustainer, internal solid motor.
Guidance: Radar command.
Range: Out to 93 miles (150km).
Flight speed: Mach 3·5.
Warhead: Blast/preformed-splinter frag (usual) or nuclear, with command detonation.

An outgrowth of the Nike Ajax, Nike Hercules became operational with the US Army in 1958. It uses a large high-performance missile and an extensive array of ground installations which detect, interrogate and track the target, track the launched missile, drive the two into coincidence and detonate the large warhead. US Army batteries were deactivated by 1974 except for a few in Alaska, southern Florida and Fort Sill (for training US and many foreign operating personnel). The replacement has for ten years been planned to be Patriot.

Right: The US Army still operates a few Nike Hercules batteries overseas, though none has served in the US since the 1970s. Though some NATO Nike Hercules installations are being updated, generally US installations are to be replaced by Patriot.

Above: Three Improved Hawks are prepared for test launch in Butzbach, West Germany. These missiles can engage aircraft at altitudes from below 100ft to over 38,000ft (30.5 to 11,582m) in all weathers and up to 25 miles (40km) range.

Patriot, MIM-104

Type: Advanced mobile battlefield SAM system.
Dimensions: Length 209in (5·31m); body diameter 16in (40·6cm); span 36in (92cm).
Launch weight: 2,200lb (998kg).
Propulsion: Thiokol TX-486 single-thrust solid motor.
Guidance: Phased-array radar command and semi-active homing.
Range: About 37 nautical miles (68·6km).
Flight speed: About Mach 3.
Warhead: Choice of nuclear or conventional blast/frag.

Originally known as SAM-D, this planned successor to both Nike Hercules and Hawk has had an extremely lengthy gestation. Key element in the Patriot system is a phased-array radar which performs all the functions of surveillance, acquisition, track/engage and missile guidance. The launcher carries four missiles each in its shipping container, from which it blasts upon launch. Launchers, spare missile boxes, radars, computers, power supplies and other items can be towed or self-propelled. Patriot is claimed to be effective against all aircraft or attack missiles even in the presence of clutter or intense jamming or other ECM. Fundamental reasons for the serious delay and cost-escalation have been the complexity of the system, the 1974 slowdown to demonstrate TVM (track via missile) radar guidance, and inflation. Unquestionably the system is impressive, but often its complication and cost impresses in the wrong way and the number of systems to be procured has been repeatedly revised downwards. The authorized development program was officially completed in 1980, when low-rate production was authorized. In 1983 production was cautiously being stepped up and the first operational units were formed in mid-1983. The US Army plans to have 81 Patriot batteries, for which its hardware requirements are 103 fire units and 4,273 missiles.

Right and below: Test launches of Patriot missiles. This system is being procured by the West Germans as well as the US Army and will play a significant role in NATO battlefield and air defense operations.

113

Redeye, FIM-43A

Type: Shoulder-fired infantry surface-to-air missile.
Dimensions: Length 48in (122cm); body diameter 2·75in (7cm); span 5·5in (14cm).
Launch weight: 18lb (8·2kg); whole package weighs 29lb (13kg).
Propulsion: Atlantic Research dual-thrust solid.
Guidance: Initial optical aiming, IR homing.
Range: Up to about 2 miles (3·3km).
Flight speed: Mach 2·5.
Warhead: Smooth-case frag.

The first infantry SAM in the world, Redeye entered US Army service in 1964 and probably 100,000 had been delivered to the Army and Marine Corps by 1970. It has severe limitations. It has to wait until aircraft have attacked and then fire at their departing tailpipes; there is no IFF. Flight speed is only just enough to catch modern attack aircraft and the guidance is vulnerable to IRCM. Engagement depends on correct identification by the operator of the nature of the target aircraft. He has to wait until the aircraft has passed, aim on a pursuit course, listen for the IR lock-on buzzer, fire the missile, and then select a fresh tube. The seeker cell needs a cooling unit, three of which are packed with each missile tube.

Right: Each combat-arms battalion in Europe has a Redeye section with four to six teams, now being re-equipped with Stinger.

Stinger, FIM-92A

Type: Portable air-defense missile.
Dimensions: (Missile) length 60in (152cm); body diameter 2·75in (7cm); span 5·5in (14cm).
Launch weight: 24lb (10·9kg); whole package 35lb (15·8kg).
Propulsion: Atlantic Research dual-thrust solid.
Guidance: Passive IR homing (see text).
Range: In excess of 3·1 miles (5km).
Flight speed: About Mach 2.
Warhead: Smooth-case frag.

Developed since the mid-1960s as a much-needed replacement for Redeye, Stinger has had a long and troubled development but is at last in service. An improved IR seeker gives all-aspect guidance, the wavelength of less than 4·4 microns being matched to an exhaust plume rather than hot metal, and IFF is incorporated (so that the operator does not have to rely on correct visual identification of oncoming supersonic aircraft).

To rescue something from the Roland program, Boeing has developed a container for four Stinger missiles which fits the Roland launch tube, though this had not entered production by 1983. In FY 1981 the first 1,144 missiles for the inventory were delivered at $70·1m, and totals for 1982 and 1983 were respectively 2,544 at $193·4m and 2,256 at $214·6m. Total requirements for the US Army and Marine Corps are currently some 17,000 fire units and 31,848 missiles.

An improvement program entitled Stinger-POST (Passive Optical Seeker Technique) is now in hand. This operates in both the ultra-violet and infra-red spectra, the combination of the two frequency bands giving improved discrimination, longer detection range, and greater ECCM options.

Right: Whereas Redeye is limited to stern chase, Stinger permits effective attack from all angles, and is more resistant to ECM.

Sergeant York, M998

Type: Divisional air-defense gun (DIVAD).
Crew: 3.
Armor: Hull, as for M48A5; turret, rolled homogenous armor steel.
Dimensions: Length (hull) 22ft 7in (6·882m); width 11ft 11in (3·631m); height (turret roof) 8·15ft (2·484m); height (antenna) 11·28ft (3·439m).
Combat weight: Approximately 60 tons.
Armament: Twin 40mm L/70 Bofors automatic guns.
Performance: As for M48A5.

For many years NATO armies have envied the Soviet ZSU-23-4 self-propelled air-defense gun, in which a proven 23mm quad MG was married to a valve-technology radar and mounted on an existing chassis to produce one of the most effective current air-defense systems. The US Army seems at last to have heeded this object lesson in cost-effectiveness with the Sergeant York DIVAD. ▶

Right: The M998 Sergeant York DIVAD, showing M48 chassis.

Below: An existing tank chassis, the Bofors L70 gun, and the F-16 fighter radar combine to give an effective AD gun system.

▶ The US Army's main problem lay in deciding just what kind of forward air-defense system it needed: gun, missile, or a mix? Once it was decided that a gun was required, there followed many studies on caliber, type and number of tubes per chassis. The process began in 1962 and it was not until 1977 that the Army asked industry to submit proposals, using the M48A5 chassis and as much "mature, off-the-shelf" equipment as possible. The resulting competition was won in 1981 by Ford, who combined a twin Bofors L/70 installation with a radar developed from that used on the F-16 fighter, on the M48 chassis. First delivery took place in 1983 and the first battery will be fielded in 1985. Total requirement is 618 fire units.

The Bofors L/70 gun, in wide service throughout NATO, is both effective and extremely reliable. Two combat rounds will be used: a pre-fragmented proximity-fuzed HE round for use against aircraft; a point-detonating round for use against ground targets. Maximum slant range against aircraft is about 9,843ft (3,000m) and maximum ground range is some 4,370 yards

Above: The Sergeant York system is produced by Ford and the total Army requirement is 618 fire units; first fielding scheduled for 1985.

(4,000m). 502 rounds are carried for each gun and combined rate of fire is some 620 rounds per minute.

The radar automatically determines target type, assigns priorities and updates the fire control unit which automatically aligns the turret and guns. The Identification Friend-or-Foe (IFF) fitted has 90 per cent commonality with that fitted to the Stinger SAM (*qv*). Air defense engagements on the move are possible, although accuracy in this case is open to question.

The turret is intended to be mounted on the M48A5 chassis, although most early production will be on M48A1 or M48A2 chassis, re-engined and with new transmissions. This is because all M48A5 chassis are currently required for active US Army units, for the National Guard, or for operational reserve stocks.

US Roland

Type: Forward area air-defense missile.
Dimensions: Length 94·5in (240cm); body diameter 6·3in (16cm); span 19·7in (50cm).
Launch weight: 143lb (65kg).
Propulsion: Internal boost and sustain solid motors.
Guidance: Initial IR gathering followed by semi-active radar command to line-of-sight.
Range 3·73 miles (6km).
Flight speed: Burnout velocity Mach 1·6.
Warhead: 14·3lb (6·5kg), contains 65 shaped charges each with lethal radius of 20ft (6m); prox fuze.

Below: A US Roland air-defense missile is fired from its tracked launcher, discarding sabots as it leaves the launch-tube. After a prodigiously expensive conversion program the US Army has decided to procure only one battalion's worth, mounted on a wheeled launcher.

Originally developed as a mobile battlefield system with plain optical (clear-weather) guidance, Roland has from 1969 onwards been further developed as Roland 2 with blindfire radar guidance. The missile has folding wings and is fired from a launch tube on a tracked vehicle, the US Army carrier being the M109. Decision to buy Roland was taken in 1974, but the introduction to Army service has been affected by prolonged technical difficulties and cost overruns, and no American Roland was fired until the end of 1977. The cost of developing the US system escalated by several hundred per cent, and after prolonged delays the decision was taken to cancel the program, even though production had already begun. The 27 fire units and 595 missiles will therefore be utilized by a light air defense battalion of the New Mexico National Guard, with a combat mission in the third echelon of the Rapid Deployment Force. Further, the fire units, instead of being mounted on the M975 tracked carrier, will now be mounted on an M812 5-ton truck chassis.

It is a somewhat humiliating end to a program which was once hailed as a great European breakthrough into the American weapons market. It also leaves a major deficiency in the US Army's low-level air defense capability.

Vulcan, M163/M167

Type: 20mm Vulcan air defense system.
Crew: 1 (on gun).
Weight (firing and traveling): 3,500lb (1,588kg).
Length traveling: 16ft (4·9m).
Width traveling: 6·49ft (1·98m).
Height traveling: 6·68ft (2·03m).
Elevation: −5° to +80°.
Traverse: 360°.
Effective range: 1,750 yards (1,600m).
(*Note: specification refers to the towed version.*)

The 20mm Vulcan is the standard light anti-aircraft gun of the US Army and has been in service since 1968. There are two versions of the Vulcan system in service, one towed and the other self-propelled; both are fair weather, daylight only systems. The towed version is known as the M167 and this is mounted on a two wheeled carriage and is normally towed by an M715 or M37 truck. When in the firing position the weapon rests on three outriggers to provide a more stable firing platform. The self-propelled model is known as the M163 and this is mounted on a modified M113A1 APC chassis, the chassis itself being the M741. The latter will be replaced by the twin 40mm Sergeant York DIVAD (*qv*).

The 20mm cannon used in the system is a modified version of the air-cooled six-barrel M61 Vulcan cannon developed by General Electric. It is also the standard air-to-air cannon of the US Air Force. The Vulcan cannon has two rates of fire, 1,000 or 3,000 rounds per minute, and the gunner can select either 10, 30, 60 or 100 round bursts. The M163 has 500 rounds of linked ready-use ammunition while the self-propelled model has 1,100 rounds of ready-use ammunition.

The fire control system consists of an M61 gyro lead-computing gun sight, a range-only radar mounted on the right side of the turret (developed by Lockheed Electronics), and a sight current generator. The gunner normally visually acquires and tracks the target while the radar supplies range and range rate data to the sight current generator. These inputs are converted to proper current for use in the sight. With this current the sight computes the correct lead angle and adds the required super elevation.

The turret has full power traverse and elevation, slewing rate being 60°/second, and elevation rate being 45°/second. Power is provided by an auxiliary generator.

The Vulcan air defense system is normally used in conjunction with the Chaparral SAM. Each Vulcan/Chaparral battalion has 24 Chaparral units and 24 self-propelled Vulcan systems. Airborne and Airmobile divisions

Above: M167A1 is the towed version of Vulcan; this uses linked ammunition whereas SP version fires electrically primed linkless.

have a total of 48 towed Vulcan systems. The Vulcan system is normally used in conjunction with the Saunders TPQ-32 or MPQ-49 Forward Area Alerting Radar, which provides the weapons with basic information such as from which direction the targets are approaching.

The 20mm cannon has a maximum effective slant range in the anti-aircraft role of 1,750 yards (1,600m). It can also be used in the ground role, and was deployed to Vietnam for this purpose; in this role it has a maximum range of 4,920 yards (4,500m). A variety of different types of ammunition can be fired, including armor piercing, armor piercing incendiary, and high-explosive incendiary. The weapon is also produced for export without the range-only radar. All American M167 VADS now have dual road wheels for improved stability.

Below: Range and lethality of the six-barreled gun are considered inadequate, and the Army will replace Vulcans with the twin 40mm Sergeant York DIVAD from 1985. There are 379 M163s and 221 M167s in service.

Below left: Tracked version of the Vulcan is M163A1 on converted M113 chassis. Combat loaded its cruising range is some 275 miles (440km).

Anti-Tank Weapons

The great tank versus anti-tank battle continues to be waged, with the advantage swinging from one side to another every few years. With the advent of new types of protection such as the British "Chobham armor", the traditional hollow-charge warhead must inevitably become of ever-decreasing value, although it will remain effective against

Copperhead, M712

Type: Cannon-launched guided projectile (CLGP).
Dimensions: Length 54in (1·37m); diameter 155mm.
Launch weight: 140lb (63·5kg).
Propulsion: Fired from gun.
Guidance: Laser homing.
Range: 1·9-10 miles (3-16km).
Flight speed: Supersonic.
Warhead: Shaped charge, 49·6lb (22·5kg).

Conventional artillery, when used in the indirect fire role, has a 1-in-2,500 chance of killing a tank. The US Army started a high-risk program to develop a projectile which could be fired from a standard 155mm weapon (for example, the M109A1 self-propelled gun or the M198 towed howitzer) and hit targets over 7·5 miles (12km) away.

Basic research proved that the project was possible and contracts were awarded to Texas Instruments and Martin Marietta. Each company built a small number of projectiles (designated Cannon-Launched Guided Projectiles) which were tested at the White Sands Missile Range. The Martin Marietta CLGP scored direct hits on both stationary and moving tanks at ranges of 5-7·5 miles (8-12km). The projectile hit the target despite deliberate aiming errors of several hundred metres. In September 1975 a CLGP hit a stationary M48 tank 5 miles (8km) away while the target was being illuminated by a laser carried in a Praeire IIA RPV. The RPV located the target with a TV camera, focusing on the target, and signalled the artillery to

Right: Tripod-mounted version of AN/TVQ-2 laser locater designator which could be used with Copperhead AT missiles.

Below: The extremely accurate and highly destructive Copperhead AT missile demonstrates its killing capabilities on an M47 on test.

older types of tanks for as long as they remain in service. The new armors must, however, pose a serious problem for the infantry, for whom the hollow-charge rocket-propelled missile provides an excellent lightweight and accurate short-range anti-tank weapon. For heavier anti-tank weapons, the immediate future seems to lie with top-attack and the penetration of the currently less well protected upper surfaces—to which the tank designers' reply will doubtless be thicker armor. A first attempt at such a weapon—Copperhead—has not been a total success, and it may be some years before second-generation top-attack weapons are proved to be really viable weapons systems.

---

fire a CLGP. As a result of these trials, Martin Marietta was awarded a contract for full scale development of the CLGP.

The basic idea is that a forward observer sees an enemy tank approaching. He then radios its approximate position to the artillery and one weapon fires a CLGP in the general direction of the target. Once the CLGP is on its way the forward observer illuminates the target with his Ground Laser Locator Designator (or GLLD), the CLGP senses the reflected laser energy and, by applying commands to its control fins, flies into the laser spot on the target. It can be steered into the target provided the nominal gun-aiming point is

within about 0·7 miles (1·1km) of it. Copperhead is treated like any other gun ammunition.

There has been exceptional cost escalation in the Copperhead program, rising from an estimated $5,500 per round in FY 1975 to $37,632 in FY 1982. This, coupled with the realization that the M712 is not so wonderful a weapon as once was thought, has led to a drastic curtailment of the program. Production ceased in 1982 when 8,750 rounds had been made, and these will serve only in artillery units assigned to the RDF. Copperhead will not be used by the US Army in Europe, nor will the once-planned European production consortium be formed. The program that was once claimed to herald an artillery "revolution" is thus coming to an expensive and somewhat ignominious end.

Dragon, M47, FGM-77A

Type: Infantry anti-tank/assault missile.
Dimensions: Length 29·3in (74cm); body diameter 4·5in (11·4cm); fin span 13in (33cm).
Launch weight: 24·4lb (11· 1kg.
Propulsion: Recoilless gas-generator thruster in launch tube; sustain propulsion by 60 small side thrusters fired in pairs upon tracker demand.
Guidance: See text.
Range: 200 to 3,300ft (60-1,000m).
Flight speed: About 230mph (370km/h).
Warhead: Linear shaped charge, 5·4lb (2·45kg).

Dragon was designed as a medium-range complement to TOW (*qv*). In service since 1971, Dragon comes sealed in a glass-fiber launch tube with a fat rear end containing the launch charge. The operator attaches this to his tracker comprising telescopic sight, IR sensor and electronics box. When the missile is fired its three curved fins flick open and start the missile spinning. The operator holds the sight on the target and the tracker automatically commands the missile to the line of sight by firing appropriate pairs of side thrusters. The launch tube is thrown away and a fresh one attached to the tracker. The Army and Marine Corps use the basic Dragon, while developments involve night sights and laser guidance.

The Dragon system is not without its problems. Perhaps the most important is that the missile body diameter of 4·5in (11·4cm) sets the limit on the size of the warhead. The effectiveness of a shaped charge warhead is a function of its diameter, and at least 6in (15cm) is likely to be needed to counter the new armors coming into service on the latest Soviet tanks. In addition, the missile is slow; this aggravates the difficulties of the operator, who must hold his breath throughout the flight of the missile. The operator is also adjured to grasp the launch-tube tightly, for if he does not his shoulder may rise at the moment of launch, thus sending the missile into the ground. Finally, the rocket thrusters have been found to deteriorate in storage, and many need replacement.

Initial plans for a Dragon replacement centered on a program designated IMAAWS, but this was halted in 1980. The new program is called Rattler and is scheduled to start development in FY84.

Tank Breaker

Type: Fire-and-forget anti-tank missile.
Dimensions: Length 43in (1·09m); body diameter 3·94in (100mm).
Launch weight: Complete system under 35lb (15·8kg); missile 20lb (9· 1kg).
Propulsion: Boost/sustain solid motors.
Guidance: Staring focal-plane array IR.
Range: About 2,187 yards (2,000m).
Flight speed: Transonic.
Warhead: Shaped charge.

One of the first weapons to use a focal-plane array, an advanced imaging IR seeker, Tank Breaker is a one-man portable missile which can be locked-on to a tank, helicopter, low-performance fixed-wing aircraft, or other target, and fired. It will thereafter home by itself, the operator having previously programmed it either to fly a direct course or (against armor) plunge down from above. This overhead attack technique has become necessary because the frontal and side armor on modern tanks will defeat a shaped-charge warhead carried by a missile of this size.

Above: Dragon is useful, if limited: it seems the gunner must avoid blinking while aiming; the missile is considered slow, short of range and not particularly effective against "new armor".

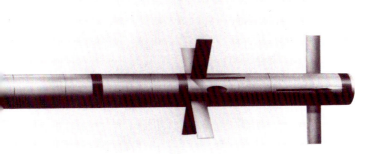

Above: Tank Breaker could allow the gunner to fire the missile and then either take cover immediately or engage another target.

TOW, BGM-71

Type: Heavy anti-tank missile.
Propulsion: Hercules K41 boost (0·05s) and sustain (1s) motors.
Dimensions: Length 45·75in (1,162mm); body diameter 6in (152mm); span (wings extended) 13·5in (343mm).
Launch weight: (BGM-71A) 46·1lb (20·9kg).
Range: 1,640 to 12,300ft (500 to 3,750m).
Flight speed: 625mph (1,003km/h).
Warhead: (BGM-71A) Picatinny Arsenal 8·6lb (3·9kg) shaped-charge with 5·3lb (2·4kg) explosive. See text for later.

The TOW (Tube-launched, Optically-tracked, Wire-guided) missile is likely to set an all-time record in the field of guided-missile production. Prime contractor Hughes Aircraft began work in 1965 to replace the 106mm recoilless rifle. The missile's basic infantry form is supplied in a sealed tube which is clipped to the launcher. The missile tube is attached to the rear of the launch tube, the target sighted and the round fired. The boost charge pops the missile from the tube, firing through lateral nozzles amidships. The four wings indexed at 45° spring open forwards, and the four tail controls flip open rearwards. Guidance commands are generated by the optical sensor in the sight, which continuously measures the position of a light source in the missile relative to the LOS and sends steering commands along twin wires. These drive the helium-pressure actuators working the four tail controls in pairs for pitch and yaw. In 1976 production switched to ER (Extended-Range) TOW with the guidance wires lengthened from ▶

Right: From left, the three main members of the family—TOW, I-TOW (Improved) and the larger TOW-2 now in production.

Below: The TOW gunner needs only to keep the sight cross hairs on target to score a hit at up to 12,300ft (3,750m). Thermal imaging infrared night sights are also included.

▶ 9,842ft (3,000m) to the figure given. Sight field of view reduces from 6° for gathering to 1·5° for smoothing and 0·25° for tracking. The missile electronics pack is between the motor and the warhead.

TOW reached IOC in 1970, was used in Vietnam and the 1973 Middle East war, and has since been produced at a higher rate than any other known missile. The M65 airborne TOW system equips the standard American attack helicopter, the AH-1S TowCobra and the Marines' twin-engine AH-1J and -1T Improved SeaCobra, each with a TSU (Telescopic Sight Unit) and two quad launchers. Other countries use TOW systems on the BO 105, Lynx, A109, A129, 500MD and other attack helicopters.

In late 1981 production began of the Improved TOW, with a new warhead triggered by a long probe, extended after launch to give 15in (381mm)

stand-off distance for greater armor penetration. The shaped-chargehead, with LX-14 filling and a dual-angle deformable liner, is also being retrofitted to many existing rounds.

Hughes is now producing TOW 2, which has several I-TOW improvements, plus a new warhead with the same diameter as the rest of the missile with a mass of 13lb (5·9kg) and an even longer (21·25in, 540mm) extensible probe, calculated to defeat all tanks of the 1990s. Flight performance is maintained by a new double-base motor giving about 30 per cent greater total impulse, and the command guidance link has been hardened.

Below: TOW has been used on a wide range of mounts, including Jeep, tripod, armored vehicles, and many helicopter types.

Small Arms

US Army small arms have been repeatedly dragged into the domestic political arena, since they represent a comprehensible part of the American frontier ethos. Having forced its NATO allies first to 7·62mm and then to 5·56mm caliber, the US Army now finds itself with the M16 unable to make optimum use of the actual 5·56mm round adopted by NATO. Repeated efforts to find a replacement for the

M16A1

Type: Rifle.
Caliber: 5·56mm.
Length overall (with flash suppressor): 38·9in (99cm).
Length of barrel: 19·9in (50·8cm).
Weight (including 30-round loaded magazine): 8·2lb (3·72kg).
Range (maximum effective): 300 yards (274m).
Rate of fire: 700-950rpm (cyclic); 150-200rpm (automatic); 45-65rpm (semi-automatic).
Muzzle velocity: 3,280ft/s (1,000m/s).

The M16 (previously the AR-15) was designed by Eugene Stoner and was a development of the earlier 7·62mm AR-10 assault rifle. It was first adopted by the US Air Force, and at a later date the US Army adopted the weapon for use in Vietnam. When first used in combat numerous faults became apparent and most of these were traced to a lack of training and poor maintenance. Since then the M16 has replaced the 7·62mm M14 as the standard rifle of the United States forces. To date over 5,000,000 have been manufactured, most by Colt Firearms and the weapon was also made under licence in Singapore, South Korea and the Philippines. Twenty-one

Below: An M16 being used during training with the Multiple Integrated Laser Engagement System (MILE).

Below right: An M16 fitted with the M203 40mm grenade launcher which has a range of up to 382 yards (350m).

venerable M1911A1 0·45in pistol have been frustrated by the US Congress; this elderly (to put it kindly!) handgun fires a round which is not NATO standardized, although the US Special Forces, and especially Delta, think highly of its stopping power at short ranges. The M60 is widely used but is being progressively replaced by a Belgian light machine gun—an excellent example of the "two-way street", but regarded as something of an affront by some elements of the US "establishment". One factor still to be addressed is the infantry's predilection for "prophylactic" fire, which is expensive in ammunition and logistic resources, and unlikely to be effective in European conditions.

---

armies use the M16. The weapon is gas-operated and the user can select either full automatic or semi-automatic. Both 20- and 30-round magazines can be fitted, as can a bipod, bayonet, telescope and night sight. The weapon can also be fitted with the M203 40mm grenade launcher, and this fires a variety of 40mm grenades to a maximum range of 382 yards (350m). The M203 has now replaced the M79 grenade launcher on a one-for-one basis. The Colt Commando is a special version of the M16 and this has a shorter barrel, flash supressor and a telescopic sight, reducing the overall length of the weapon to 27·9in (71cm). The M231 is a special model which can be fired from within the M2 Bradley Infantry Fighting Vehicle.

There has been consistent dissatisfaction with the M16A1 in the US Army, and even more so in the other main user—the US Marine Corps. One of the major complaints is its lack of effectiveness at ranges above 340 yards (300m), which has come to a head with the increased emphasis on desert warfare with the RDF. This, combined with the high average age of current stocks, led to a major review in 1981.

As a result, a "product improved" weapon (M16A2) is now under consideration. A major feature would be a stiffer and heavier barrel, utilizing one-turn-in-seven-inches (17·8cm) rifling—as opposed to one-turn-in-twelve-inches (30·5cm)—to enable the new standard NATO 5·56mm (0·218in) round to be fired. Other features under consideration are a three-round burst capability to replace the current full-automatic, an adjustable rearsight, and a modified flash eliminator. The opportunity would also be taken to introduce tougher "furniture", ie, butt-stock, pistol grip, and handguard.

A program is in hand to examine new technologies for incorporation in a possible future weapon. These include controlled-burst fire and multiple projectiles (eg, flechettes).

M1911A1

Type: Pistol.
Caliber: 0·45in (11.43mm).
Length: 8·63in (21·93cm).
Length of barrel: 5·03in (12·78cm).
Weight loaded: 2·99lb (1·36kg).
Weight empty: 2·49lb (1·13kg).
Effective range: 65ft (20m).
Muzzle velocity: 826ft/s (252m/s).

The 0·45 caliber M1911 pistol was the standard American sidearm of World War I. In 1923, work on an improved model commenced at Springfield Armory, and this was standardized as the M1911A1 in 1926, and since then the weapon has been the standard sidearm of the US Army. The Army does, however, use other pistols for special missions, as the M1911A1 is rather heavy and has quite a recoil. Between 1937 and 1945, over 19 million M1911A1 pistols were manufactured by Colt, Ithaca and Remington. The weapon is semi-automatic, and all the user has to do is to pull the trigger each time he wants to fire. The magazine, which is in the grip, holds a total of seven rounds. The fore sight is of the fixed blade type and the rear sight consists of a U notch on dovetail slide. The weapon has three safety devices: the grip safety on the handle, the safety lock, and the half cock position on the hammer.

Manufacture of the M1911A1 ceased in 1945 and the cost of spare parts, especially barrels and slides, is becoming very high. This, combined with a number of operational shortcomings (such as the heavy recoil), and the lack of commonality with the standard NATO 9mm round, has led to a long search for a replacement. This resulted in a 1982 shoot-off between four competing designs: the US Smith & Wesson 459M, the Swiss-German SIG-Sauer P226, the German Heckler & Koch P7A13, and the Italian

M60

Type: General purpose machine gun.
Caliber: 7·62mm.
Length: 43·3in (110cm).
Length of barrel: 22in (56cm).
Weight: 23lb (10·48kg) with bipod; 39·6lb (18kg) with tripod.
Maximum effective range (bipod): 984 yards (900m).
Maximum effective range (tripod): 1,968 yards (1,800m).
Rate of fire: 550rpm (cyclic); 200rpm (automatic).

The M60 is the standard GPMG of the US Army and has now replaced the older 0·30 Browning machine gun. The weapon was developed by the Bridge Tool and Die Works and the Inland Division of General Motors Corporation, under the direction of Springfield Armory. Production of the M60 commenced in 1959 by the Maremont Corporation of Saco, Maine.

The M60 is gas-operated, air-cooled and is normally used with a 100-round belt of ammunition. To avoid overheating the barrel is normally changed after 500 rounds have been fired. Its fore sight is of the fixed blade type and its rear sight is of the U-notch type and is graduated from about 656ft to 3,937ft (200 to 1200m) in about 328ft (100m) steps. The weapon is provided with a stock, carrying handle and a built in bipod. The M60 can also be used on an M122 tripod mount, M4 pedestal mount and M142 gun

Right: The M60 can be fired from the hip, shoulder, bipod or a variety of mounts for use on aircraft and vehicles.

Above: There are well over 400,000 M1911A1s in US service, each of them overhauled an average of three times. An unusually accurate marksman could make this elderly self-loading pistol effective up to 160 yards (50+m).

Beretta 92SB. All four failed the test in one way or another and, as a result, in February 1982 Congress prohibited the use of any further funds in projects involving a 9mm handgun. It would, therefore, appear that the famous "45" will soldier on for many years to come.

mount for vehicles. Other versions include the M60C remote for helicopters, M60D pintle mount for vehicles and helicopters and the M60E2 internal model for AFVs.

The M60 will remain in service with the US Army for many years. It is sturdy, reliable, and highly effective.

M2 HB

Type: Heavy machine gun.
Caliber: 0·50in (12·7mm).
Length overall: 65·07in (165·3cm).
Length of barrel: 44·99in (114·3cm).
Weight (gun only): 83·33lb (37·8kg); 127·8lb (57·98kg) with tripod.
Range: 1,996 yards (1,825m) effective in ground role; 7,470 yards (6,830m) maximum; 820 yards (750m) anti-aircraft role.
Rate of fire: 450/575rpm.

The 0·50 caliber M2 machine gun was developed for the US Army in the early 1930s, as the replacement for the 0·50 M1921A1 MG. The weapon was developed by John Browning (who designed many other famous weapons including the Browning Automatic Rifle and the Browning 0·30 machine gun), and the Colt Firearms company of Hartford, Connecticut.

The M2 is air-cooled and recoil operated, and is fed from a disintegrating metallic link belt. The weapon can fire either single shot or full automatic, and various types of ammunition can be fired including ball, tracer, armor-piercing and armor-piercing incendiary. For ground targets the weapon is mounted on the M3 tripod while for the anti-aircraft role the M63 mount is used. It is also mounted on many armored fighting vehicles including the M113A1 series of APC (and variants), the M109/M108 SPH and the M578 and M88 ARV. The M55 anti-aircraft system (no longer in service with the US Army) has four M2s, and the M2 is also mounted in helicopters and in some commanders' turrets as the M85. The M2 HB MG is still being produced in the United States by Ramo Incorporated and the Maremont

M72A2

Type: Light anti-tank weapon (LAW).
Caliber: 66mm.
Length of rocket: 20in (50·8cm).
Weight of rocket: 2·2lb (1kg).
Muzzle velocity: 476ft/s (145m/s).
Maximum effective range: 355 yards (325m).
Length of launcher closed: 25·7in (65·5cm).
Length of launcher extended: 35in (89·3cm).
Weight complete: 4·75lb (2·15kg).

The M72 is the standard Light Anti-Tank Weapon (LAW) of the US Army and is also used by many other armies around the world. Development of weapon started in 1958 with the first production LAWs being completed by the Hesse Eastern Company of Brockton, Massachusetts, in 1962. It is also manufactured under licence in Norway by Raufoss. The LAW is a light-weight, shoulder-fired rocket launcher and its rocket has a HEAT warhead which will penetrate over 11·8in (300mm) of armor. It can also be used against bunkers, pillboxes and other battlefield fortifications.

When the M72 is required for action, the infantryman removes the safety pins, which open the end covers, and the inner tube is telescoped outwards, cocking the firing mechanism. The launcher tube is then held over the shoulder, aimed and the weapon fired. The launcher is then discarded. Improved models are known as the M72A1 and the more recent M72A2.

The successor to the M72A2 was to be the Viper, which was supposed to be so cheap and effective that it was planned to issue it to virtually every man in the front line. Weighing a little under 9lb (4·1kg), Viper has a 2·75in (70mm) diameter warhead with a performance against modern Soviet armor that is marginal, to say the least. Following strong criticism by the

Above: The M2 HB on M3 tripod. It is fed from a 100-round dis-integrating-link belt at a cyclic rate of fire of 450-575 rounds a minute.

Corporation, and it remains in service in some 20 countries.

 The M2 HB went out of production shortly after World War II, but the line was recently re-opened, mainly, but not entirely, for export sales. The letters "HB" in the designation stand for "hydraulic buffer", a modification introduced in the late 1930s.

Above: Effective range of LAW against stationary "soft" targets is 355 yards (325m), and less than half that against moving targets.

General Accounting Office (GAO), the US Congress ordered a shoot-off between Viper and three European weapons: the British LAW 80, the Norwegian M72-750, and the Swedish AT4. A further complication arose when General Dynamics refused to sign a fixed-price contract for Viper. The US Army is thus faced with either buying a European LAW system off-the-shelf or soldiering on with the M72A2 until a better US-designed successor is available.

M79

Type: Grenade launcher.
Caliber: 40mm.
Weight of grenade: 0·610lb (0·277kg).
Length of launcher: 29in (73·7cm).
Length of barrel: 14in (35·6cm).
Weight of launcher: (empty) 5·99lb (2·72kg); loaded, 6·5lb (2·95kg).
Muzzle velocity: 249ft/s (76m/s).
Range: 437·4 yards (400m) maximum; 383 yards (350m) effective, area targets; 164 yards (150m) effective, point targets.
Effective casualty radius: 5·46 yards (5m).
Rate of fire: 5 rounds per minute.

The 40mm M79 Grenade Launcher was developed to give the infantryman the capability to deliver accurate firepower to a greater range than could be achieved with a conventional rifle grenade. The M79 is a single shot, break-open weapon and is fired from the shoulder. It is breech loaded and fires a variety of different types of ammunition including high explosive, high explosive air burst, CS gas and smoke. Its fore sight is of the blade type and its rear sight is of the folding leaf adjustable type. The latter is graduated from 82 yards (75m) to 410 yards (375m) in about 27 yards (25m) increments. When the rear sight is in the horizontal position, the fixed sight may be used to engage targets up to 109·3 yards (100m). The M79 has been replaced in front line units by the M203 grenade launcher which is fitted to the standard M16A1 rifle.

M249

Type: Squad automatic weapon (SAW).
Caliber: 5·56mm.
Lengths: Overall 39·4in (100cm); barrel 18·5in (47cm).
Weights: Empty 15·5lb (7·03kg); with 200-round magazine 22lb (9·97kg).
Effective range: 1,421 yards (1,300m).
Rate of fire: 750rpm.
Muzzle velocity: 3,033ft/s (924m/s).

The SAW idea was conceived in 1966, but it has taken a long time to reach service. When the M16 was issued to infantry squads, all infantrymen had an automatic weapon, but with a maximum effective range of some 330 yards (300m) only. It was considered that each fire team in the squad needed a weapon of greater all-round capability than the M16, but obviously not a weapon as heavy or as sophisticated as the M60. The SAW meets this requirement, and will be issued on a scale of one per fire team, ie, two per squad. The SAW may also replace some M60s in non-infantry units.

The M249 SAW is a development of the Belgian Fabrique Nationale (FN) "Minimi". Current orders are being met from the FN factory, but it is intended to set up a production line in the USA. Current requirements are for 26,000 M249s for the Army and 9,000 for the Marine Corps in a five-year program, but further orders will doubtless follow.

The M249 is very smooth in operation and displays a reliability that is considered exceptional in light machine guns. Fully combat ready, with a magazine of 200 rounds, bipod, sling, and cleaning kit, the M249 weighs 22lb (9·97kg), which is still 1lb (0·4kg) less than an empty M60 machine gun. The M855 ball round fired from the M249 will penetrate a US steel helmet at a range of 1,421 yards (1,300m).

Overall, the M249 is superior to the Soviet PKM 7·62mm (bigger, heavier, smaller mag), and the RPK 5·45mm (bigger, lighter, smaller mag).

Above: Largely replaced now by the M203/M16A1 rifle combination, the M79 fires the full range of 40mm grenades.

Above: The M249, which is better than the M16, especially at extended ranges. It is left-hand fed from a 200-round container.

Vehicles

Far less glamorous and eye-catching than tanks or armored personnel carriers, there is a vast range of support and logistic vehicles vital to any modern army. Some of these vehicles are simply adapted for the particular environment of the battlefield, such as passenger-carrying vehicles which are "ruggedized" and fitted with four-wheel drive.

Hummer

Type: High mobility, multi-purpose wheeled vehicle (HMMWV).
Dimensions: Length 15ft (4·57m); width 7ft (2·15m); height 5ft 9in (1·75m).
Weights: Empty 4,969lb (2,254kg); maximum 8,532lb (3,870kg).
Engine: General Motors V-8, 6·2 liter diesel, 130hp at 3,600rpm.
Performance: Maximum road speed 65mph (105km/h); road range 351 miles (565km); gradient 60 per cent.

Modern armies are very dependent upon wheeled vehicles of all types, and perhaps the most important of these is the field car; exemplified in the US Army by the ubiquitous Jeep and in the British Army by the Land Rover. The quantity of vehicles needed is enormous, and the importance of the Hummer can be gauged from the fact that some 40,000 will be bought by the US Army, with a further 11,000 going to the USAF and 14,000 to the USMC.

A "drive-off" was held in 1982 for the three competitors for this lucrative contract, the winner being American Motors General. Following the

There are also, however, numerous types of highly specialized vehicles, ranging from recovery trucks ("wreckers") through ammunition delivery and ambulances to bridging launchers, and just a very few selected types are shown here. It is doubtful whether even the US Army knows how many vehicles it possesses, but the scale of numbers may be assessed from the fact that the new commercial utility ¾-ton truck is the subject of an order for 53,248 vehicles (most for the Army, but some for the other services) with an option for a 100 per cent increase. Planned procurement for the US Army and USMC on just four new types of vehicle amounts to $1,704 million in Fiscal Year 1985.

announcement of this success in March 1983, AM General was bought by the ever-growing LTV Corporation for $170 million. Production has begun and first deliveries are due in 1984.

The Hummer is intended by the US Army to replace several vehicles: the early model M151 quarter-ton Jeep; M274 half-ton Mule; M880 1¼-ton pick-up truck; M561 Gama Goat articulated utility vehicle; and M792 1¼-ton ambulance. The Hummer has four road wheels driven through geared hubs, enabling the vehicle to be no more than 5ft 9in (1·75m) high and thus bettering the design requirement of 6ft (1·82m). Considerable attention has been paid to a comfortable ride and to weight saving. Some 18 variations on the design are already planned, ranging from a simple pick-up to ambulances and a TOW missile launcher.

With its massive US order-book and its clear potential for large-scale overseas sales, there is no doubt that the Hummer is destined to become as familiar as its famous predecessor, the Jeep.

Below: The versatile Hummer will be used in the airborne, airmobile and light infantry division as TOW missile carrier, and will also be used for recce, fire support, communications, command and control.

M60 (AVLB)

Type: Armored vehicle-launched bridge.
Crew: 2 (commander; driver).
Armament: None.
Armor: Front 4in-4·72in (101-120mm); sides 2in (51mm).
Dimensions (vehicle): Length 28ft 4in (8·648m); width 12ft (3·657m); height 10ft 4in (3·162m).
Weight (vehicle): 91,900lb (41,685kg).
Engine: Continental AVDS-1790-2A, 12-cylinder diesel; 750bhp at 2,400rpm.
Performance: Road speed 30mph (48·28km/h); range 310 miles (500km); fording 4ft (1·22m); gradient 60 per cent; vertical obstacle 3ft (0·91m); trench 8ft 6in (2·59m).

The US Army's requirement for a tactical bridge is met by the M60 AVLB, although numbers of M48 AVLBs remain in service. So far as is known, there are no current plans to develop an AVLB version of the M1.

The M60 AVLB can use a variety of bridges. The first weighs 31,900lb (14,470kg) and is made of aluminum. It is 63ft (19·2m) long and can span a gap of 60ft (18·3m), taking 3 minutes to launch and from 10 to 60 minutes to recover (depending on the ground). The second bridge weighs 19,000lb (8,618kg), has an overall length of 92ft 10in (28·3m), and can span 88ft 7in (27m). Both have a Bridge Classification of Type 60; ie, they will take a load of 60 tons.

Other types of bridging used by the US Army include the Mobile Assault Bridge/Ferry (MAB) and the British-designed Medium Girder Bridge (MGB).

Below: The highly mobile M60 chassis without turret, fitted with a hydraulic cylinder assembly and a scissors bridge.

Above: An M113 mounted with Vulcan air defense system trundles across an AVLB emplaced by the M60 chassis parked on the bank.

M88A1

Type: Medium armored recovery vehicle.
Crew: 4 (commander, driver, co-driver, mechanic).
Armament: One 0·50 M2 HB machine gun.
Dimensions: Length (without dozer blade): 27·15ft (8·267m); width 11·24ft (3·428m); height with anti-aircraft machine gun 10·58ft (3·225m).
Weight: 111,993lb (50,800kg).
Ground pressure: 1·63lb/in^2 (0·74kg/cm^2).
Engine: Continental AVSI-1790-2DR diesel engine developing 750bhp at 2,400rpm.
Performance: Road speed 26mph (42km/hr); range 280 miles (450km); vertical obstacle 3·49ft (1·066m); trench 8·58ft (2·61m); gradient 60 per cent.

The standard medium armored recovery vehicle used by the US Army in the early 1950s was the M74. This was based on a Sherman tank chassis but could not handle the heavier tanks which were then entering service. In 1954, work on a new medium armored recovery vehicle commenced and three prototypes, designated the T88, were built by Bowen-McLaughlin-York. After trials, a batch of pre-production vehicles was built and then Bowen-Laughlin-York were awarded a production contract for the vehicle which was standardized as the M88. Just over 1,000 M88s were built between 1961 and 1964, and some were also exported abroad. The M88 uses many automotive components of the M48 tank, and can recover AFVs up to and including the M60 MBT. Its role on the battlefield is to recover damaged and disabled tanks and other AFVs, and it can, if required, remove major components from tanks such as complete turrets. When the M88 first entered service it was armed with a 0·50 caliber machine gun mounted in a turret but this was subsequently replaced by a simple pintle mounted 0·50 machine gun.

The hull of the M88 is of cast armor construction and provides the crew with protection from small arms fire and shell splinters. The crew compartment is at the front of the hull and the engine and transmission are at the rear. A hydraulically operated dozer blade is mounted at the front of the hull and this is used to stabilize the vehicle when the winch or "A" frame is being used, and can also be used for normal dozing operations. The "A" type frame is pivoted at the front of the hull, and when not required this lies in the horizontal position on top of the hull. This frame can lift a maximum load of

Above: The M88A1 can recover every type of AFV in the US Army inventory, including the M1 Abrams. Here the A frame used to remove and change major components, such as complete turrets, is seen stowed to the rear of the vehicle.

six tons (5,443kg), or 25 tons (22,680kg) with the dozer blade in the lowered position.

The M88 is provided with two winches and both of these are mounted under the crew compartment. The main winch is provided with 200ft (61m) of 32mm cable and has a maximum pull of 40 tons, whilst the secondary winch, which is used for hoisting operations, has 200ft (61m) of 16mm cable. The vehicle is provided with a full range of tools and an auxiliary fuel pump. This enables the vehicle to transfer fuel to other armored vehicles.

All M88s of the US Army have now been brought up to M88A1 standard and are fitted with the Continental AVDS-1790-2DR diesel engine developing 750bhp at 2,400rpm. This gives the vehicle a longer operating range of 280 miles (450km) compared to the original M88. It is also fitted with an APU and can also be fitted with a NBC system. Current production model is M88A1 which has also been exported to many parts of the world.

Below: Early M88 kitted out for deep water fording tests. M88A1 is expected to operate in all types of terrain in all weathers.

M578

Type: Light armored recovery vehicle.
Crew: 3.
Armament: One 0·50 M2 HB machine gun.
Dimensions: Length overall 21ft (6·42m); width 10·331ft (3·149m); height with machine gun 11·20ft (3·416m).
Weight: 53,572lb (24,300kg).
Ground pressure: 1·56lb/in² (0·71kg/cm²).
Engine: General Motors Model 8V71T eight cylinder liquid diesel developing 425bhp at 2,300rpm.
Performance: Road speed 34mph (54·71km/h); range 450 miles (725km); vertical obstacle 3·3ft (1·016m); trench 7·76ft (2·362m); gradient 60 per cent.

In the mid-1950s, the Pacific Car and Foundry Company of Renton, Washington, was awarded a contract by the US Army to build a new range of self-propelled artillery, all of which were to use the same common chassis. These three weapons were the T235 (which eventually entered service as the 175mm M107), the T236 (which entered service as the 8inch M110) and the T245 (this was a 155mm weapon but was not developed past the prototype stage). In 1957, it was decided to build a range of light armored recovery vehicles using the same chassis as the self-propelled guns. Three different prototypes were built. Further development resulted in the T120E1 which had a diesel engine, and this entered service as the M578.

The first production M578 was completed by the FMC Corporation in 1962, and since then the vehicle has been produced by the designers, Pacific Car and Foundry, and more recently by Bowen-McLaughlin-York. Between FY 1976 and FY 1978, the US Army requested some $64 million to purchase an additional 283 M578s.

The M578 is used by all arms, including self-propelled artillery battalions, mechanized infantry battalions, and armored cavalry regiments. Apart from recovering such vehicles as the M110 and M109, the vehicle is also

used to change major components in the field, such as engines, transmissions, and tank barrels.

The hull of the M578 is identical to that of the M107 and M110 self-propelled guns, with the driver being seated at the front of the hull on the left side and the engine to his right. The crane is mounted at the rear of the hull and this can be traversed through a full 360 degrees. The commander and mechanic are seated in the turret and a standard 0·50 Browning M2 HB machine gun is mounted on the roof for anti-aircraft protection. The crane can lift a maximum of 13·38 tons (13,600kg) and the main winch is provided with 229ft (70m) of 25mm cable. This has a maximum capacity of 26·57 tons (27,000kg). A large spade is mounted at the rear of the hull to stabilize the vehicle when the winch or crane is being used; in addition, the suspension can be locked out if required. Unlike most MBTs, the M578 is not provided with a NBC system and it has no amphibious capability. Infra-red driving lights are normally fitted.

Above: The M578 is designed to recover vehicles up to 66,137lb (30,000kg), and therefore could recover the Army's SPGs and APCs (and engines, gun barrels and so on), but not main battle tanks (the M1 weighs 120,000lb/54,432kg). The tow-winch capacity is 60,000lb (27,216kg) bare drum, and hoisting capacity is 15,000lb (6,804kg). Besides the driver there are a commander and a mechanic, who normally enter the turret through side doors, although there are also double doors at the rear. They each have a single-piece hatch cover and six periscopes. A machine gun mounted in front of the left hatch cover is provided for use against attacking aircraft. The M578 uses the M110 chassis; there are no variants in service.

M992 FAASV

Type: Field artillery ammunition support vehicle (FAASV).
Crew: 9 (maximum).
Armament: One 0·5in Browning M G.
Dimensions: Length overall 22ft 3in (6·7m); width 10ft 10in (3·295m); height 10ft 7½in (3·24m).
Weights: Loaded 57,500lb (26,082kg); cargo capacity 18,920lb (8,582kg).
Engine: Detroit Diesel Model 8V71T, 8-cylinder turbocharged diesel; 405bhp at 2,350rpm.
Performance: Road speed 35mph (56km/h); road range 220 miles (354km); vertical obstacle 1ft 9in (0·53m); trench 6ft (1·83m).

Many armies are searching for an answer to the ammunition resupply problem created by the ever-increasing capability of modern artillery. This problem has a number of facets. First, most artillery is now on highly mobile self-propelled tracked chassis, and is thus able to move more often, faster, and to more inaccessible sites. Secondly, rates of fire are increasing and

Inset: M992 will support M109 and M110 battalions in Europe from 1985. Note armored overhead protection provided by rear door.

Below: Capable of carrying 48 8in (203mm) rounds for the M110A2 SP howitzer, the highly-mobile FAASV will speed up rates of fire.

thus creating a greater quantitative requirement. Finally, increases in caliber have led to larger and heavier rounds which are more difficult for the "ammunition numbers" to handle.

The US Army's solution to this problem is the FAASV, which entered production in 1983, with introduction to service scheduled for 1985-86. The FAASV is based on the well-proven M109A2 chassis, but with a large armored housing in place of the turret. This housing contains removable vertical racks which are hoisted aboard by a 1,500lb (680kg) capacity, extendible-boom crane on the front of the vehicle. On arrival at the gun position, projectiles and charges are removed from these racks by an automatic stacker, assembled, fuzed, and then passed by an hydraulic conveyer directly into the supported gun.

The FAASV can carry 90 155mm projectiles and charges, or 48 8in rounds. The rate of passing rounds to the guns is 8 rounds per minute, which handsomely exceeds current rates of fire. An additional feature is that the armored rear door swings up to provide overhead protection during the transfer process.

This very promising vehicle is designed and built by Bowen-McLaughlin-York and 144 units are currently on order, although the US Army's requirement is for at least 250 units.

Mines

The mine is a weapon which seems always to be on the verge of a major comeback, but never quite making it. There is no doubt as to its value in at least delaying (if not actually stopping) either armored or infantry advances or deployments. The major problem, however, is the time taken to lay

---

GEMSS
Ground-Emplaced Mine-Scattering System

All NATO armies are seeking to enhance their ability to stop and defeat armored thrusts by the numerically superior Warsaw Pact forces. To this end, all forms of anti-tank weapons are being developed, and over the past decade there has been a marked revival of interest in anti-tank mines: interest both in the effect of the mines themselves and in rapid methods of laying them. The Ground-Emplaced Mine-Scattering System (GEMSS) is particularly effective, since it is mounted on a trailer that can be towed by any suitable tracked (M548 cargo carrier, M113 APC) or wheeled (5-ton truck) prime mover. GEMSS's primary purpose is quickly to lay minefields that will force attacking enemy armored vehicles into constricted areas where they will provide a rewarding target for killing weapons.

   GEMSS is the M128 mine dispenser, holding up to 800 4lb (1·8kg) mines which are deployed at intervals of 32 or 64 yards (30 or 60m), the

mines, assuming that it is most unlikely that any will be laid in peacetime. Thus, great efforts have been devoted to rapid minelaying systems, using either mechanical layers or helicopters. Much attention is also being paid to delivering large quantities of very small mines ("minelets"), using artillery shells or missiles as the delivery agent.

The full range of US Army mines covers the spectrum from small anti-personnel mines, through anti-tank mines, to the Atomic Demolition Mines (ADMs) which will soon be withdrawn from Western Europe where they have been deployed for many years. The mine is an ideal defensive weapon—provided that it can be laid in time.

interval being determined by the rate of launch and the speed of the vehicle. The M128 dispenser is mounted on the M794 trailer.

The mines are laid on the surface and a 2,734 yard (2,500m) field can be laid in less than six hours. The anti-tank mine has a magnetic influence field; this means that it can attack the whole width of the target and does not need to be run over by the tracks. There is also an anti-personnel mine, a fragmentation weapon activated by automatically deployed trip-wire sensors. Both types of mine have anti-disturbance devices to inhibit clearance, but both also have a built-in self-destruct device which neutralizes the minefield after a pre-determined interval.

Fiftynine GEMSS units were procured by the US Army in FY 1982 and a further 52 units in FY 1983.

Below: The Army's FASCAM (family of scatterable mines) program is designed to lay minefields rapidly to force enemy armor into "ambush" situations. It includes GEMSS (below) as well as mine systems seeded by artillery and aircraft.

Uniforms and Personal Equipment

The uniforms of the United States Army must cover every military requirement, from formal parades at the White House, through combat in any possible condition of terrain or climate, to fatigues and NBC warfare. The Army has usually managed to meet these requirements although, like all soldiers, the American always thinks that someone else has something just that little bit better. There has been a perceptible change in some areas. There has, for example, been a gradual increase in the wearing of berets, as the merits of this ubiquitous item of military headgear have been realized. Also, a barrack uniform of olive-green trousers and the now virtually universal woolen pullover has been adopted, a relaxed form of day-to-day wear which originated with the British Army and its "wooly pully".

The olive-drab fatigues formerly intended to be worn in combat have been replaced by a properly camouflaged outfit, with basic colors and patterns varied for different climates, from European temperate to African desert. Materials are also more up-to-date, and in addition to being more weather-proof also incorporate a certain degree of resistance to chemicals and infra-red detection. Special combat clothing is available for extremes of climate, such as Arctic or jungle environments.

Above: Paratrooper of 1st/502d Infantry, 101st Airborne Division, in desert combat uniform, in the Sinai Multinational Force, 1983.

Left: A soldier of 4th Infantry Division decontaminating his over-shoes in a special bath. Note the detection paper on his left sleeve.

A recent introduction is the new "military helmet". This was the result of years of research and much agonized appraisal. The helmet is made of laminated Kevlar and weighs only 51oz (1·45kg). It is much more resistant to projectiles than the previous model. Its most obvious characteristic, however, is its shape—the principal aim being to avoid the notorious and widely recognizable shape of the German World War II helmet. Despite this, the new helmet, especially with its camouflage cover, does bear a resemblance to the German helmet, and this led to some comment during the first use of the new headwear during the freeing of Grenada. ▶

▶ Web equipment has evolved gradually over the years, but even the Americans have not yet found a really satisfactory answer to the problem of providing a really comfortable method of carrying the impedimenta needed by a modern soldier. As was discovered by British infantrymen during the 1982 war in the Falklands, an APC or truck will not always be available to carry it all.

Much publicity is given to the overpressure systems now being fitted to all AFVs to ensure a degree of NBC protection for the crew. The vast majority of soldiers on the modern battlefield will, however, not have such protection, and will still have to rely on respirators and protective suits. In the early 1980s, the US Army found itself so lacking in this area that it had to buy some 200,000 British Mark 3 NBC suits and boots for US troops in Western Europe, to cover the gap pending issue of new American equipment. What still has to be determined—and not just by the US Army—is just how long soldiers will be able to continue fighting and working in such conditions, because nobody can pretend that wearing the full NBC equipment for protracted periods is anything other than a very trying experience.

Most US Army uniforms and items of personal equipment are well-designed and popular with the troops. There has been a noticeable increase in the smartness and bearing of American soldiers since the bad days of the aftermath of Vietnam, and they now—especially since the success in Grenada—appear proud and confident once again, which bodes well for their many allies around the world.

Below: US Army infantrymen on exercise in northern Norway move equipment on a Norwegian "pulk". This is just one of the very many deployment options for which the Army is constantly training.

Above: An infantry soldier in his combat suit and boots, holding an M16 rifle. The helmet is the new model, made of Kevlar, which is lighter, more comfortable, and offers better protection.

Radars and Communications

In any future conflict one of the major battlefields will be an invisible one—the electromagnetic spectrum—but the outcome will be crucial to overall success. Today's sophisticated, highly mobile, rapidly moving armies are totally dependent upon radars and telecommunications systems for their survival; inevitably, none more so than the US Army.

Currently, the US Army uses tactical radio systems based on the traditional radio nets using the High Frequency (HF) and Very High Frequency (VHF) bands, with some specialized needs (eg, ground-to-air) using even higher bands. A major program is now under way for the Single-Channel Ground and Airborne Radio Subsystem (SINCGARS-V) which will provide the next generation of sets. These will be light in weight, secure, and will use the most modern microprocessor techniques. They will be capable not only of voice transmissions, but also of passing data, an ever-increasing requirement on today's battlefield. The most interesting aspect, however, is that a technique known as "frequency hopping" will be used to provide a major degree of Electronic Counter-counter Measure (ECCM) protection. This means that the set transmits on any one frequency for only a micro-second at a time. For an enemy, therefore, the intercept problem becomes very acute, although the technique is not without its problems at the transmitting end as well.

As with other major armies, the US Army is putting a major effort into developing a Maneuver Control System (MCS) to provide a field commander and his staff with automated assistance in controlling the battle. The long-term system will be known as Sigma, and is likely to be very sophisticatd indeed. Currently in service are a microcomputer called the Tactical Computer Terminal (TCT) and a rather more powerful device, the Tactical Computer System (TCS). One particular device under development would put the entire battlefield map into the data base, which would not only give a picture similar to that of a current paper map, but would also give a 3-D picture from any point on the map in any requested direction. Thus, a commander would be able to "look" at his positions from the enemy's viewpoint, a unique capability.

The major strategic communications system for the US Department of

Defense is the Defense Satellite Communication System (DSCS), and the Army is responsible for developing, procuring, and operating the earth terminals. This involves equipment of many kinds, ranging from huge stations with antenna dishes several hundred feet in diameter to the latest vehicle-borne tactical terminals.

The command, control, and communications (C^3) areas are becoming ever more sophisticated, and ever more demanding in manpower and resources. There is no doubt that modern forces need a major control effort, and that the amount of intelligence and information flowing in the system is growing at a great rate as sensors become more effective; but some are beginning to feel that the limit is being approached.

The US Army also uses a great variety of radars and other electronic sensors. These range in size and role from the small, tripod-mounted infantry radars such as the AN-PPS-15 to large gun- and mortar-locating and air-defense radars. The gun- and mortar-locating radars are of especial importance to the Army in central Europe for their contribution to countering the massive fire support capability of the Warsaw Pact. Such radars can pinpoint an enemy round within seconds of its leaving the barrel, analyse its trajectory and backplot to the point of origin, and then pass the information to the counter-battery gun positions before the round has landed.

Far left: AN/MPQ-50 pulse-acquisition radar being set up by men of 38th Air Defense Artillery Brigade in Korea.

Left: An infantry company commander using a VHF radio command link. Such forward nets are simple to intercept.

Below: US Army operator using teleprinter GRC-12 radio link.

General Logistics and Resupply

According to legend, a US Army general was being briefed on the then newly discovered "science" of logistics in the early 1940s. After listening for some time with increasing bewilderment he got to his feet and said to his staff: "I still don't know what these goddam logistics are—but, whatever they are, make sure I get a lot of them!" Any logistician would say that the attitudes of commanders and their operations staffs have changed little over the years: they still do not want to be bothered with the details, but heaven help the logistics specialist who fails to deliver the goods. The US Army's logistics problem is severe, because virtually any operation will be mounted at a very considerable distance from the Continental USA. Some of these can be carefully planned and prepared for in peace; eg, West Germany or South Korea, where in-place units are supported by a well-prepared logistic system. Other deployment options are recognized but are subject to peacetime limitations; for example, the Norwegians will not permit troops or stores to be positioned on their soil in peacetime. Finally, there are the open options, such as those facing the Rapid Deployment Force.

One of the logistic problems which causes US military planners most concern is the air/sea bridge across the North Atlantic, over which, in the early days of any future conflict or crisis, vast amounts of men and materiel would have to flow. The great increase in strength of the Soviet Navy is a direct threat to these plans, and, as in World War II, some of the most crucial battles will be fought in the open expanses of the Atlantic.

A second major logistic problem facing the US forces in Europe is that in peacetime the French will not permit US military stores to be landed in, or transported across, Metropolitan France. These stores must instead be

Above: A vehicle-mounted 25-ton crane on road test for the US Army. This is one of many thousands of support vehicles of differing types necessary to a modern army.

Left: M60 tanks are unloaded from a ship. US supply lines must use the vulnerable routes across the Pacific and Atlantic Oceans; this constitutes a major risk.

landed at North Sea ports and then moved by road and rail south to the US areas along a supply route which is parallel to—and dangerously near—the Inner German Border. This is a bad situation to be in, although it must be hoped that in war the French would relent. Further in-theater problems would arise in war with the roads being crammed with refugees and vehicles trying to move in the opposite direction to the military units and supplies.

One of the major logistic problems in terms of commodities is likely to be fuel. There has recently been a major switch-over to diesel to reduce demand—but there are vast numbers of vehicles and the allied logistic services are going to be very hard pressed to meet the demands. Obviously, reserves exist, but these would not sustain a war effort for very long. Thus, the fuel resupply lines back across the oceans to the point of production will be crucially important and, again, the Soviet Fleet seems poised to threaten all these

A further problem for the logistic services in a future war will be that of dealing with casualties, especially those from chemical, biological, or nuclear attack. This is a task of awesome proportions.

OTHER SUPER-VALUE MILITARY GUIDES IN THIS SERIES......

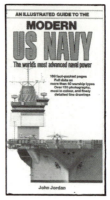

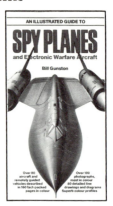

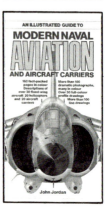

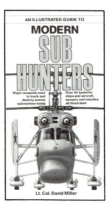

OTHER ILLUSTRATED MILITARY GUIDES NOW AVAILABLE.

Air War over Vietnam
Allied Fighters of World War II
Bombers of World War II
German, Italian and Japanese Fighters
of World War II
Israeli Air Force
Military Helicopters
Modern Fighters and Attack Aircraft

Modern Soviet Air Force
Modern Soviet Navy
Modern Submarines
Modern Tanks
Modern Warships
Pistols and Revolvers
Rifles and Sub-Machine Guns
World War II Tanks

* Each has 160 fact-filled pages
* Each is colourfully illustrated with hundreds of action photographs
  and technical drawings
* Each contains concisely presented data and accurate descriptions
  of major international weapons
* Each represents tremendous value

If you would like further information on any of our titles please write to:

Publicity Dept. (Military Div.), Salamander Books Ltd.,
27 Old Gloucester Street, London WC1N 3AF